Christian Living

in the World

by

Jay E. Adams

TIMELESS TEXTS
Woodruff, SC

Contents

Key to Abbreviations
for the Four Senses of "World"

np	non-personal world
p1	personal world, people in general
p2	personal world, Satan's Kingdom
p3	personal world, Gentiles & Jews together (contrasted with Jews only)

(see page 3 for more details)

INTRODUCTION

Many years ago I wrote a book (still in print) entitled *Christian Living in the Home*. At that time I determined to follow that volume with others along similar lines, dealing with the various relations that a Christian must sustain to those living around him. The present volume was the second that I conceived. The writing of it, however, was delayed by a number of considerations, most of which took me far afield. Yet, from the back of my mind, from time to time, thoughts about the need for this volume continued to pop forward. Now, after many years, by God's grace, I have attempted to fulfill this long-awaited task. I trust that the result will have been worth the wait.

Christians are, as the Apostle Paul made quite clear, going to have to live in a world of sin that is oriented toward sin and that is used by the Prince of this World to attempt to drag them into sin (I Corinthians 5:10). Neither the Roman Catholic monk nor the Protestant monk-like believer, holed up in his Christian bubble, escapes the world. That is an impossibility. Obviously, withdrawal from the world is no answer; there is no place to withdraw. Within one's self he carries a bit of the world wherever he goes—both that part of it to which he as a not yet totally sanctified person contributes, and that which he has imbibed from without and retains.

The world is always with you, around you and within you. For better or for worse, you live in the world. Since that is true, it is incumbent upon you as a Christian to understand what the world is, how God expects you to relate to it, and what He has provided for you to be able to do so successfully. Those matters are among the principal concerns of this book.

Early in life, young Christians ought to be taught how to relate to the world in the home, in Christian schools and in church. Certainly, if they are not given explicit direction in these matters by those who seek to raise them in the nurture and admonition of the Lord, the world will indoctrinate them. It is my hope that this book will find acceptance in each of these arenas.

By means of its many avenues of communication, the world floods its views into unsuspecting souls who are receptive to them because they have not been adequately warned and fortified against worldly propaganda. Along with what little instruction is given, often there is virtually no help for dealing with the world's powerful propaganda machines. The propaganda of the world is everywhere—on TV, throughout the internet, in magazines, on the radio and in the "music" of the day. Its messages are loud and clear. The biblical counter message must, therefore, be presented even more powerfully and must give "no uncertain sound."

If you are to be heard over the many siren voices of the world, you must be firm, sure and clear in what you say. The world's messages resound day and night from every quarter. Unless you are aware of this and are prepared to refute them with truth that rings true, the world will so quickly drag away your children and loved ones that you may find it too late to reach them. *Christian Living in the World* has been designed to help you think through these matters in a biblical fashion. Though I have stressed the need for early training because prevention is always best, this book is for all believers, of all ages and in all sorts of situations. Remedial work cannot be done too quickly.

It is my conviction that a simple, yet eminently biblical book of this sort has been needed for quite some time. Whether or not this volume is that book, and will meet the need, is for you and others like yourself to determine. My hope and prayer is that it will contribute much to keep believers—young and old alike—from naively drifting along with the flow.

Jay E. Adams
Enoree, SC 1998

Chapter One

WHAT IN THE WORLD?

The word "world" in the title of this book presupposes some knowledge of biblical terminology and usage. It is a knowledge that most Christians think they possess, but when you question them about it, many give evidence that they do not. Let me ask you, for instance, how you reconcile John 3:16, "God so loved the world," with God's command in I John 2:15, "Do not love the world?" Are you not to love what God loves? Do *you* have a satisfactory answer? Is it a problem you never faced before? Probably. If so, it begins to appear that matters are more complex than at first it seems, doesn't it? Take another two verses: "I am not praying for the world" (John 17:9) and "He is the appeasing sacrifice for . . . [the sins] of the whole world" (I John 2:2). How do you explain the apparent contradiction that Jesus prays for only *some* but is the appeasing sacrifice for the *whole*? The answers to these, and a number of other similar questions will, I trust, become clear in what follows.

Let's begin with an overview of the biblical uses of the word "world." Understanding here is essential to all else. The word is used 247 times in the [NASV] Bible, in 212 verses. It is, therefore, a significant term. Like many other terms that occur frequently, it is used in more than one sense. Indeed, there are at least four senses that the Scripture writers gave to the word. These are the *material, **non-personal** world,* the *general, **personal** world* (all the people in the world with no reference to whether they are saved or not), the ***personal** world consisting of Satan and his kingdom* (arrayed against God and His people), *and the **personal** Gentile and Jewish world combined* (as contrasted with Jews only).

The trick is to discover to which of these four references a writer is referring when he uses the word "world." Most of the time the referent is clear; sometimes the word could possibly apply to two or more of the four. In a few instances it is difficult to say to which it applies. To complicate matters further, some writers (notably John, who by "world" refers to all four referents) employ the term to express all of the four ideas without flagging changes in meaning for the reader. In one verse, for instance, it seems that John uses three of the four meanings (John 1:10).

To save confusion I shall refer to each of these four senses as follows: non-personal (*np*); personal general (*p1*); personal satanic (*p2*); personal Gentile (*p3*). So, in the reference in the last paragraph (John 1:10), the three referents included would be "He was in the world" (probably *p1*), "and the world was made by Him" (*np*), but "the world didn't know Him" (*p2*). From now on, for the sake of brevity and clarity, I shall refer to each of these uses (as I understand them) by these distinguishing labels. A table for convenient reference is included on page v.

The following chart, which by no means is exhaustive, provides samples of each use according to categories. Considering each verse should convince and acquaint you with the distinguishing features of the biblical usage.

A. The Non-Personal World

1. The physical creation: rivers and stones, but also nonhuman living creatures such as plants, animals, microorganisms—and bugs.
2. Sample verses: II Samuel 22:16; Psalm 18:15; 50:12; 89:11; 90:2; 97:4; Proverbs 8:26; Isaiah 34:1; Jeremiah 10:12; Nahum 1:5; Matthew 13:35; 16:26; Mark 14:9; John 21:25; Acts 17:24 (and many more).

B. The Personal World (in three senses)

1. Human beings in all their relationships to God, the creation and to one another.
2. *p1*
    a. People in general, living everywhere on this planet; everybody, without exception
    b. Sample verses: John 7:4; 10:36; 11:27; 12:19; 14:19; 16:21, 28; 17:6; 18:20, 36; Acts 17:6; 19:27; Romans 3:6; 3:19; I Corinthians 14:10; I Timothy 3:16; James 2:5; II Peter 3:6.

   3. *p2*

      a. Satan's Kingdom, composed of the unsaved, organized by the evil one over against God and His people. Often, the persecuting world.

      b. Sample verses: Isaiah 13:11; Matthew 18:7; John 1:10; 7:7; 12:31; 14:30; 15:18, 19; 16:8, 11, 33; 17:15; Romans 12:2; I Corinthians 1:20, 21, 27, 28; 2:12; 3:19; 11:32; II Corinthians 4:4; Galatians 4:3; 6:14; Ephesians 2:2; Colossians 2:20; II Timothy 4:10; James 4:4; I Peter 5:9; I John 2:15; 3:1, 13; 4:1, 4, 5.

   4. *p3*

      a. Gentiles and Jews together (contrasted with Jews only)

      b. Sample verses: John 1:9, 29; 3:16, 17; 4:42; 12:47; Romans 11:12; I Corinthians 7:34; I John 2:2.

Throughout the book I shall develop each of these categories, relating it in various ways to the problems of Christian living. It should be clear that the way you should relate to various aspects of the world will be different according to whether you are facing the *np*, *p1*, *p2* or *p3* world. A thorough understanding of these matters should help you to become more sure-footed in dealing with the world in *all* of its dimensions. Often the problem is simply not knowing what in the world is going on. My purpose is to help enlighten you. During your brief journey in this world, the goal is to become *God's* World Class Citizen!

Chapter Two

THEY'RE WORLDS APART

In this chapter I shall discuss the world as a material, non-personal creation. That does not mean, however, that the matters we shall consider will be less than personal in nature. The believer must relate to this non-personal "world." That opens up the possibility that the discussion may become intensely personal. Indeed, before I have completed the chapter, there may be some who have become widely divided over what I am about to say in a highly personal, even emotional manner. It is nearly impossible to consider the non-personal world impersonally!

It is, then, the world considered in its material—organic and physical—aspects *apart from* the human beings who live in it (except for man's material body, as it is a part of the physical, non-personal world) that we shall be taking a look at. All of this should become clearer to you as we proceed.

When God created the world, He declared it "good; very good" (Genesis 1:31). But we know from the further account in Genesis 3 that things did not remain that way. After man sinned, the world could no longer be said to be very good. The ground grew weeds and thorns. Women now bore children in pain as men sweated to provide food to feed them. Indeed, if Adam had avoided the tree of the knowledge of good and evil and if he had eaten of the tree of life, he and his posterity would have lived forever in perfection. But that was not to be.[1] Man rebelled against his gracious Creator and brought death and destruction upon himself, upon his posterity and upon the nonpersonal creation (cf. Romans 8:18ff.). The entire creation, including the redeemed, is pictured here by the apostle Paul as a woman groaning in birth pangs as she awaits the delivery of a fresh, new world where, at once, sin and its consequences will be eliminated forever. But that glorious hope is just that—a hope—as certain as history (because it is promised by God in His Word) but, alas, not yet realized (Romans 8:25). That is why books of this sort, containing discussions about the world, are necessary.

We all, redeemed and unredeemed alike, live in a world that is less than good, less than perfect. It is a world, not only in which people sin, but also one in which the consequences of their sin must be dealt with daily. These are two: God's curse and man's destructiveness. The problem for the Christian, who understands the biblical dynamics behind this fact of a sin-cursed, sinning world, is *how* to do so.

Obviously, the believer cannot escape the world (though some persons have thought that they could by various means. Consider, for instance, the suicide

---

1. For details, see my book *The Grand Demonstration*, in which I thoroughly discuss the matter.

cult that recently tried to follow the Hale-Bopp comet). But closer to home, neither can the conservative Christian escape into the "Christian bubble."[1] Note how Paul expresses disdain for all such ideas in relation to the *p2* world in I Corinthians 5:9[b]. The same sentiment is every bit as true with reference to the *np* world. So, he must learn to live *in* it, in relationship *to* it. The practical challenge to him is—*how*?

There are, of course, siren voices aplenty telling him how. There are the environmentalists and the animal rights activists, both of whom at times tend to put the non-personal above the personal. There are those who so stress nutrition or bodily exercise that they have turned proper concerns for the physical body into cultic rites and rituals. Not only have churches been split over nutritional issues, but whole denominations have insisted on vegetarianism as a canon of orthodox theology. There are abortionists and geneticists who consider it more important to preserve the human race as a herd than as individuals.

To whom is the believer to listen? How much of the propaganda that floods his ears from day to day is

---

1. Some Christians have attempted to avoid all contact with the personal (*p2*) world, and as much contact with the non-personal (*np*) world as possible by withdrawing from the presence of unbelievers, by denying themselves things and by isolating themselves in some sort of a world-pro-

he to believe and act on and how much should he reject? Do those people who fear global warming have a point? Is acid rain destroying the environment? Are snail darters and spotted owls more important than people in the industries that have been stymied in order to preserve animals and birds? Is there any truth in these crusades?

Or are the proponents of these viewpoints simply advocates of hopeless and empty causes since, not knowing the Creator, they have no *real* cause to promote? Do they unknowingly worship the creation rather than their Creator (Romans 1:25)? Are they to be avoided? Opposed?

How is the believer to relate to the newly revived cult of *Gaia* whose members openly bow down to the earth goddess? This heretical, pagan movement seems closely associated with environmentalism. Feminism also seems tightly linked to the newly-revived Gnostic religions which, contrary to the original, first century Gnostics, strangely emphasize the

---

protective bubble. Poverty, for instance, is thought by some Protestant ascetics to be an ideal because by it one reduces the number of "things" that he possesses. But see I Timothy 6:17, where God is said to "richly provide everything for our enjoyment." That is a vital truth with which ascetics must grapple. Rarely, if ever, do you read of them doing so—it might burst their bubble!

physical.[1]

These and dozens of other questions of a similar nature arise as we think of the Christian in relation to the nonphysical world in which he lives. In this chapter, I shall examine with you some of the biblical information that bears upon these issues and attempt to help you develop a sane, balanced, biblical view.

So let's begin. I suggest that we must come to understand what we mean by the words "personal" and "non-personal." I am concerned here not with scientific categories, but with a working understanding that conforms to and grows out of the biblical data. These data clearly distinguish the personal from the non-personal (*np*) world. The Scriptures are totally free from animistic views which confuse people with things. When John distinguishes the "world" from the "things that are in the world," for instance, he speaks in a manner that is utterly consistent with the viewpoint expressed throughout the Bible (I John 2:15).

What do we mean, then, by saying that a being is "personal"? "Non-personal"? Christians must understand these matters clearly in order to deal properly with the *np* world.[2]

---

1. See Peter Jones, *Spirit Wars*, (Mulkiteo) Wine Press, 1997.
2. I shall not attempt to discuss the personality of the Members of the Trinity, of the angels or of

By the term *personality* we indicate that a being bears a responsible, reasonable, person to Person relationship to his Creator, Who will judge him according to a standard that He has given to him (cf. Hebrews 9:27). That means that he has been created with knowledge, reason, a moral nature and a conscience. All of these elements which are a part of the image of God have been greatly corrupted by sin. In the regenerate, God is in the process of restoring and renewing these elements (cf. Ephesians 4:24; Colossians 3:10). Moreover, a person is in the line of Adam who came into being by means of special creation when God breathed into his nostrils the breath of life and he became a living soul (Genesis 2:7). That did not happen to the animals, the microorganisms, the viruses or the mountains and lakes which are all a part of the *np* world. The body of Adam, prior to the giving of the breath of life was nothing more than another element (though also specially fashioned in a direct and separate event by God) of the *np* world. What made him personal was the reception of the life breathed into his body. That personality resides particularly in the spirit of man is clear from the fact

---

any other nonhuman being that might exist. To range beyond the discussion of the human personality would be to go further than the scope this book allows (though you will, I hope, detect inevitable nuances in the discussion pertaining to these other personalities).

that, at death, when the spirit leaves the body (James 2:26), he continues as a person who will be judged (once more, see Hebrews 9:27). Dogs, squirrels and orangutans will not be so judged. They have no personality that lives on after death. Moreover, Peter plainly states that "irrational animals" are "naturally born to be captured and destroyed" (II Peter 2:12). By this, he makes it clear that their destiny is different from that of human beings.

The *np* world, then, consists of all that does not partake of human personality, whether it be living organisms like geraniums and skunks, or purely materialistic ones like rocks and clouds. All that is not personal is a part of the *np* world. And it is that with which this chapter is concerned.

Unmistakable biblical principles set the parameters within which we shall conduct our discussion of the Christian and the *np* world. You also may find them helpful in deciding other questions in the future. Here are some with which to begin.

1. God gave man rule over the *np* world (Genesis 1:28).
2. Man was to subdue it (or bring it into his control).
3. When the *np* world takes over, and God's order is inverted, there can be nothing but trouble (cf. one such example: Exodus 23:28, 29; Deuteronomy 7:22).
4. The *np* world participates in the curse of sin (Genesis 3:14-19).

5. God is displeased with the *np* world as it is presently constituted. He will remake it anew (Revelation 21:5).

6. The Christian relates to the *np* world by means of his body.

Recognize that man is intended to rule over the *np* world. That means that he has been given the place of dominion over the animals. It also means that, in the command to subdue the earth, through science, etc., he is to bring forth all the possibilities in the *np* world. Discovery and utilization are also involved in "subduing" (or bringing the *np* world into his control). The invention of the computer on which I am writing is an example of just such subduing. It is a technological breakthrough that previous generations had no idea could be achieved. Naturally, when a sinner subdues the world, he does so imperfectly, sinfully using it for his own ends rather than for God's glory. It wasn't long after the Internet was in place, up and running, that Internet pornography reared its slimy head. But it isn't only that man misuses the *np* world, the fact is that he abuses it as well. Every board that is nailed, is nailed imperfectly; every brick that is laid, is laid in ways that do not exactly conform to the architect's blueprint which, itself, is imperfect. A holy, perfect God is offended by these imperfections that exist in all parts and aspects of the sin-cursed *np* world. Yet, He patiently waits until the Day He has set to create a new, perfect world (II Peter 3:9-13; Revelation 21:5, 10-27). In that day, all the imperfect "works" of man will be burned up—obliterated once and for all (II Peter 3:10).

With reference to the animals over which man is to bear rule, it is certain that anyone who through his activism places man's welfare in jeopardy because of some consideration for animals has an unbiblical view of the matter. While Christians believe in treating animals well (cf. Proverbs 12:10; Jonah 4:11), they must not join with those who push man from his rightful place and instead enthrone animals under the label of "animal rights." The Bible nowhere speaks of animals having rights, but it does speak of human beings having them. And these rights extend to rule over the animal kingdom.

Vegetarianism is fine as long as the practitioner avoids meat out of preference (or, in some few cases, for medical reasons). But when a vegetarian, who squashes ants with his feet every day he walks outdoors, becomes an advocate of vegetarianism in order to bring an end to "slaughtering poor animals" for the sake of food, he (or she) is out of line biblically.[1] Not only did God explicitly give meat to man to eat (Genesis 9:2, 3), but He set up temple worship of Himself that involved the slaughter of multitudes of animals

---

1. Cf. Romans 14:2. Note, especially, what God considers the proper attitude toward such matters (vv. 3, 4). Moreover, I Timothy is a strong refutation of the vegetarian advocates.

and the *required* eating of red meat by His priests. These factors must be understood if one would attempt to understand how to relate to animal activists in our day.

Now, it is clear that no wanton, wasteful hunting should occur simply for "the sake of the kill." That would be against the practical terms in which the slaughter of animals is set forth (temple worship symbolized partaking of the coming Messiah Who would be slain for guilty sinners, and, in addition, animal flesh was eaten simply as food). Everything in the Bible is opposed to strongly-enforced philosophies of vegetarianism, despite what Seventh Day Adventists may say.

"What, then, about clean air, pollution and the like? Shouldn't we try to preserve and clean up the environment in which we live?" Of course, there is nothing wrong with doing so, *per se*. And Christians, for instance, have usually supported such reasonable projects as reforestation. But when such activities as the tree-hugging extremists advocate mean burdensome taxes on people, losses of whole industries together with their jobs, costly renovation of automobiles, then they should not be supported. Global warming, for instance, is a highly questionable theory, yet unproven. To hold conferences based on such weak evidence in order to formulate and pass restrictive laws that are burdensome and costly to people is clearly out of the question. There is more subduing to be done with reference to this matter! No one wants melting ice flows to inundate houses and lands, but scientific subduing, as of the present moment, gives no solid evidence that this will ever take place. Nor do we want dirty rivers or air, and as far as this can be helped without upsetting the order set forth in the biblical principles listed above, the Christian will participate—but never with the fanatical zeal flowing from belief that this world is all that there is or ever will be, so that, at all other costs, we must quickly attempt to achieve perfection!

But there is a very important point to be raised at this juncture. The *np* world is greatly flawed. Because they have no hope beyond what they experience in this life, many of these activists are quite frenzied in their approach to the *np* world. They have been indoctrinated with Spenserian philosophy. According to this view, progress is always possible; indeed, perfection lies just over the horizon. Activists want perfection in the areas of their concerns—and they want it now! There is the problem. The Christian knows that perfection is not attainable. There can be technological progress to a large degree, it is true, but ethical and moral? No way! Every man born into the *np* world is born a sinner who will abuse and destroy it. Apart from those few pockets where because of spiritual regeneration among the populace the moral change of a society can be seen for a time (as in Geneva where it is reported to have lasted for 200 years after Calvin), no progress in moral lifestyle can be found in history—nor will it be. Men will go on sinning and advocating sin. Is the wide-open sin of America an improvement over the more restrained sin of two generations ago? It is these contemporary sinners who advocate drugs and protect the drug culture. Are the drug culture and the movie industry today more or less destructive to the *np* world than Ozzie and Harriet TV shows? What, for example, have drugs and illicit sex done for the physical health and welfare of society?

But there is much more to be said from this angle. The Christian knows that there is no hope for the *np* world as it is presently constituted, that improvements are temporary, and that (as the verses quoted above indicate) some day God will wipe all man's works from the face of the earth as He melts it down and refashions it. He puts little trust in the political and social schemes and promises made by those who have no more hope than man's renovation of the present *np* world. They, being ignorant of God's future design for the perfect "world to come" (Hebrews 2:5) which He Himself will build, are much like the unbelieving Jews Paul spoke about when he wrote, "Out of ignorance of God's righteousness, and by trying to contrive their own, they didn't submit to God's righteousness" (Romans 10:3). What they do, they do "under the sun," as the writer of Ecclesiastes put it. That is, they do it for the here-and-now alone.

On the other hand, with the hope that is his, the Christian, along with the apostle Paul, cannot help

comparing the present world with the coming one (cf.
II Corinthians 4:17, 18). His hope is not in anything
in this world, or in what man can do. Like Abraham,
he knows that there is nothing here but that which is
temporal. He refuses to bank on what can be done in
a cleaner city here when he is longing for the "city
whose Builder and Maker is God" (Hebrews 11:10).
He cannot help but remember when things are askew
here that there is coming a time when he and the *np*
world will be freed from its "slavery to corruption"
(Romans 8:21). And whenever he makes those com-
parisons, he knows that what is here is "not worthy of
comparison" with what will be (Romans 8:18). There
the eternal city will be heavy with glory. (Nothing
will mar it—neither pollution, grime, nor dirty air—
since sin and all its effects will be removed.)

The Christian, as a result, is a pilgrim and a
stranger here; he is seeking a homeland (Hebrews
11:14). That is how the Lord Jesus seemed to operate
here in this sin-cursed world, isn't it? He healed some
of the sick (at other times he left behind some still
sick as He moved ahead to carry on His work elsewhere). There was no frenzy on His part to bring
about total healings or perfect conditions. He held
loosely all the things of this world. When He spoke
of the Christian's influence on the world He
described it as a preserving influence. He called
Christians the "salt of the earth" (Matthew 5:13). Salt
preserves. (It was used to keep fish from spoiling). It
does not make that which is already rotten fresh

again. The believer thinks about the lost *np* world as he does about lost sinners: he doesn't attempt to reform them, knowing that they need regeneration instead. Neither will he waste time and energy trying to reform a world that also needs regeneration. To be salt where he is, preventing as much sinful destruction as possible, is probably the best a believer can hope to achieve in the present *np* world.

As the apostle Paul so clearly wrote, Jesus' view of the present *np* world was quite different from that of many Christians who want to build a heaven on the present earth. Referring to such concepts, Paul wrote that the things in the *np* world are "all intended to be used up and perish" (Colossians 2:22). That's it! The Lord Jesus mounted no crusade to clean up the environment, to reform the practices of those around Him (though abortion and even infanticide were legal). Rather, He taught us to "lay up treasures in heaven" (Matthew 6:19, 20). You could put it like this: the believer is to "use up" the things in this world, all of which are perishable, for the purposes of glorifying God (the ultimate goal) and sending ahead treasures that are eternal (the proximate goal and by-product of achieving the ultimate goal). That's not bad—trading bad money for good!

That means that the Christian, while not lackadaisical about sin or its effects on the *np* world, nevertheless is not surprised at what he finds. Indeed, he expects imperfection of every sort. And like God Who plans to burn all man's works in the final conflagration (II Peter 3:10), he puts little stock in what is accomplished here. Things here, he recognizes, are for using in the present. The best one can do with them is to transform them into treasures that can neither rot, nor rust—as present wealth and possessions inevitably do.

When Adam sinned, he brought death and destruction to the human race and to the *np* world. Everything in a sin-cursed world eventually goes to pot. You keep your automobile in repair for just so long; eventually it ends up in the junk yard. You and your doctor keep you alive and functioning for just so long; eventually, the grave worms get your body. Nothing in this *np* world is permanent. Fight it as you may, the effects of sin keep crawling forward apace like kudzu.

"Is the Christian a cynic then? Is he so heavenly minded that he is no earthly good?" Absolutely not! In fact, just the opposite is true. The unbeliever, who has only the here-and-now to live for, at length becomes as frustrated and cynical as Ecclesiastes says he will. But because the Christian knows that how he relates to the present *np* world will make a difference in the eternal *np* world, he works with alacrity, laying up treasures in heaven to God's glory. He remembers I Corinthians 15 where he is urged to be "always abounding in the Lord's work, knowing that his labor for the Lord isn't worthless." Did Paul have the book of *Ecclesiastes* in mind when he wrote those words? Well, we know that the cynical concepts expressed there by one who labors for himself and for this life alone ("beneath the sun") are precisely the opposite of those truths that God through Paul is assuring the Christian.

The Christian believes in enhancing life here as he is able. He does not reject eyeglasses (or lens implants), hearing aids and the like. But he knows that all that others do is imperfect. Indeed, all he does is imperfect also. And in his mind is an on-going repentance for not being perfect as his Father in heaven is perfect (Himself complete in every way and in all He does). But he is not wedded to philosophies of progress or perfectibility, nor is he hopeful about the visions and proposals of sinners who, like rebellious Nimrod, think they can build a world empire that will reach into the heavens. He knows that the empire of God, which came with the Lord Jesus Christ, is "not of this world." He knows that the weapons Christians use are not politics, pressure groups, or force, but persuasion from the Scriptures (John 18:36; II Corinthians 10:3-6).

What is the upshot of this discussion? The Christian is to rule and subdue, to occupy and to control. But he does so within a context of sin and its effects. The consequence of this is that neither he nor anyone else can ever do anything perfectly. While striving for perfection, he must settle for perfection only in the world to come. The present world is not his hope. He believes in pie in the sky, not worth in the earth! He participates in its activities, but as one who "uses it

Chapter Three

IT'S A WIDE, WIDE WORLD

This chapter will be brief. It deals with the personal world in general. Whenever the Bible mentions the worldwide population of the earth it is speaking of what we have designated *p1*. The second half of Psalm 24:1, "the earth is the Lord's, and all it contains [*np*], the world and those who dwell on it" [*p1*], refers to the entire population of the earth. The whole world of men is said to be God's possession. This does not mean that they are His covenant people whom He calls His peculiar treasure. They are His by creation. The covenant community, the church, is His by the new creation in Christ Jesus. Every person on the globe, without exception, is commanded to fear God (Psalm 33:8). If he fails to do so, he must pass through His negative, condemning judgment. No one will escape (Psalm 96:10, 13; 98:9). Because of universal sin all—even those who are most noble in the estimation of other men—will fade away (Isaiah 24:4). These very general statements are made about the very general group that is under consideration.

Jesus' siblings urged Him to demonstrate His powers to the whole world (John 7:4). It is to the entire world—to those who don't see and those who do—that Jesus came (John 9:39). And in a bit of angry exaggeration, Jesus' enemies declare, "the world has gone after Him!" (John 12:19). Much the same was later said of the apostles: "These men who have upset the world have come here also" (Acts 17:6). The uses of the word cited in this paragraph are for purposes of exaggeration. More of this exaggeration is seen in the statement about the goddess Diana, when her devotees cry, that she is one whom "all Asia and the world worship" (Acts 19:27). His siblings say, "if you are so great, go show the whole world," His enemies complain that since many Jews were listening to Jesus the world has begun to follow Him. The disciples are dubbed with a similar, but even more negative, epithet, and the Ephesians represent their deity as being worshipped by everyone. (Cf. also I Timothy 3:16; James 2:5.)

As I said, there are but scanty references to the world as a whole. That is noteworthy in itself, since in Chapter 14 we shall be looking at passages that often are mistaken as *p1*, when in reality they are *p3* verses. There is nothing strange about the fact that the use of words like "all, everyone, the whole" are rarely used in the absolute sense. Ordinarily, they mean *all* of something, some group, a class; everyone in a group, class; the whole of something or other. That, for instance, is the case in II Peter 3:9 where Peter says that God is "not willing that *any* should perish but that *all* should come to repentance." The question is any of *whom*? All of *whom*? Surely, if God wills that none should perish but that all should repent in the *absolute* sense of those terms, then every man, woman and child who was ever conceived would be saved. God's will is not thwarted. Peter clearly does not mean that because infants can't repent. We know from other Scripture that people will suffer for eternity in hell, and that there are plenty of people who die without ever coming to repentance. So, it is clear that the "any" and the "all" in the verse must refer to any and all of a certain body of people, and not to any and all indiscriminately or comprehensively.

And that is precisely what the context makes clear. The scoffers claim that God's promises are not being fulfilled (vv. 3, 4). Peter sets forth several facts in reply: 1) they willingly forget the flood; 2) by the same Word of God which predicted the flood, the prediction of another Day of judgment has been prophesied which is just as surely coming; 3) time is not the same with God as with men (v. 8); 4) God isn't slack concerning His promise, but He is waiting patiently for every one *of you*, His elect, to come to repentance. He will not miss even a single one of His own by hurrying things up. He will patiently wait until all who are ordained to eternal life believe.

Nothing more that is helpful in understanding how Christians should live in relationship to the world of people in general is noted in the biblical material cited, so we must now turn to the next chapter which begins to deal with the *p2* world. Because the *p2* world is the Christian's principal problem it will be necessary to devote the bulk of this volume, in several chapters, to this world.

Chapter Four

WELCOME TO THE WORLDWIDE WEB

That's Satan's invitation! Like a vicious, poisonous spider, he has woven his web and in innumerable ways invites the Christian to come his way, hoping to entangle and trap him in it. All too often he is successful in this attempt. One reason is that many Christians fail to understand what is going on until it is too late. In Galatians 6:1, Paul speaks of the brother or sister who is "caught" in sin. The "catching" of another in a trespass may refer to *overtaking* or *surprising* him in the trespass, or to the fact that he is *trapped* in it.[1] Possibly, since the two meanings were equally credible translations of the word in his time, Paul had both in view as he wrote. He seems to have been thinking of Christians coming upon brothers or sisters who were so entangled in sin that they needed other Christians to help them become disentangled and "restored" since they were not extricating themselves from it. At any rate, Christians do become trapped in sinful patterns and habits. They do get

---

1. The verb *prolambano* can mean "to seize, catch, capture" (see Souter, *A Pocket Lexicon of the Greek New Testament*).

caught as the result of the devil's wiles, and thus they do give him a toehold into their lives (Ephesians 4:27). An understanding of the *p2* world and how to deal with it, therefore, is utterly essential. The subject of the *p2* world holds so important a place in the Bible and is so widely referred to that the believer must come to grips with what the Scriptures say about it if he cares to live as God wishes him to.

First, let's roughly sketch this "world" in order to make it recognizable. Everyone who has been born by natural generation comes into the *p2* world as a member of it. He is born in sin (see Ch. 1; Psalm 51:5; Romans 3:10-23). Early on he begins to develop a self-centered lifestyle. His activities all amount to nothing less than service to the kingdom of Satan. He is born into darkness (ignorant of the light and truth of God); he is born guilty and condemned (Romans 5:18, 19; John 3:18, 19); he is born dead spiritually (Ephesians 2:1ff.), and he is born a child of Satan (John 8:44). In other words, everyone by his natural birth is born into Satan's kingdom of darkness (Colossians 1:13). This means that, as a former participant in it, you should not be unfamiliar with this world (Ephesians 4:17). Until you became a believer through faith in Jesus Christ, you contributed to and fully participated in its activities. When you were "translated"[1] out of the kingdom of darkness into the

---

1. Transferred: as a colonist or exile who is transported to a different land.

Kingdom of God's dear Son, you, for the first time, began to realize that everything in your life must change (cf. Ephesians 2:3; 4:17). Since then, by the Spirit's wisdom (found in the Bible), initiative and power (Philippians 2:13; Romans 5:5) you have been involved in a process of learning to live according to the standards of this new land. You have been shedding the old life and putting on the new life of Christ.[1] But this is a life*long* process that will be completed only when at death (or the Lord's return) you will be instantaneously glorified by God Himself.

So, when describing the *p2* world, we are speaking about that large host of people who, unlike the believer, have never repented and believed the gospel. They are still in the same condition as when they were born. They are called "those without," "the unsaved," "enemies of the cross of Christ" and a host of other names in the Scriptures, all of which help identify them as a part of the *p2* world. This world, therefore, consists of all who have never been redeemed. This body of persons makes up the majority of mankind at any given time in history.[2] Although those of whom it is composed differ in

---

1. For details, see my book *Winning The War Within,* which details the problem and its solution, focusing especially on Romans 6 and 7.
2. They enter into the *wide* gate and travel the *broad* road because they are so numerous. Chris-

many other ways—such as race, creed, language, nation—it is constituted a cohesive whole by virtue of its alignment to the evil one in whose power it lies (I John 5:19). Though unrecognized by its citizens, it is an organized entity, called a "kingdom" (see above) and boasts a ruler (Ephesians 2:2; Matthew 9:34; John 12:31). Indeed, in this last passage, Satan is described as "the *prince* of this [*p2*] world." His is a kingdom utterly opposed to the kingdom of God and at war with it (cf. Genesis 3:15; Matthew 12:30).

But the devil and his kingdom have been dealt the death blow by the sacrifice of Jesus Christ (Colossians 2:13-15) who now, in their last throes, are thrashing about seeking to do as much damage as possible. An animal in that condition can be very dangerous before it finally dies. While the Christian knows that Satan's ultimate defeat is sure, he is advised to "resist" him, understand his "wiles" and "flee" from the temptations he dangles before him. There is no question, then, that if the devil "goes about as a roaring lion, seeking whom he may devour" (I Peter 5:8), the first thing the Christian ought to know is that this one and his loyal followers are his enemies, and that he is in a warfare with them. He is not to align himself with the enemy. He is to win battles in the war waged by the enemy, not lose them. He is to "be alert" and prepared to go into bat-

---

tians, on the contrary, are always in the minority and need but a *narrow* road and a *straight* gate.

tle at a moment's notice (Ephesians 6:10-18). As Calvin put it, he is to stand with one foot raised at all times. That is the first thing that he should know about the world we are considering.

Because it is Satan's world, he is furious with you for becoming a traitor and going over to his Enemy. He does not take kindly to that. Consequently, he will give you as much trouble as he can. You should not think that this life will be an easy one: "In the world you will suffer persecution." That is a part of Christian living in the world. The persecution may not be physical (as it has been in the past and still is in many parts of the world) but, in one form or another, it will come if you "live in a godly manner for Christ Jesus" (II Timothy 3:12).

Should Christians fear Satan, then? Is it possible for him to place thoughts in your mind, to control you, to possess or oppress you? No. The consistent message of the New Testament is that the demons[1] fear the Savior and His followers (e.g., see Mark 5:7). While the evil one can sorely tempt, he cannot "touch" the believer (I John 5:18). What he did to Job, only under special permission from God and in divinely-proscribed ways, is not possible for him to do to you, believer.[2] The words in I John 5 are a great

---

1. Demons are fallen angels who followed Satan in his rebellion against God. They now serve him.
2. The word used here for "touch" is the same Greek term used in the Septuagint in Job 1:12; 2:5.

comfort. You should not be afraid of the devil; he should fear you, assuming that you are living as you should. The One in you is greater than the one who is in the world (I John 4:4). That is an important and powerful thought to keep in mind. If ever you lose a battle with the devil and his hosts, it is because you have failed to properly depend upon and draw upon the power of the One within you, the Spirit of Christ.

But though this is true, the world (that is, the group composed of people who belong to Satan's kingdom) is dangerous, as we said. It persecutes. It also tempts. And there is still much of the world that clings to the believer. Though he has been snatched from the fire, he yet smells of smoke (Jude 23). Indeed, when James speaks of temptation, he doesn't even mention Satan's temptation; rather, he refers to the habituated desires within believers (James 1:14).

Because prior to your salvation you yielded the members of your body to sin leading to further sin (Romans 6:19) and you became habituated to those activities, you must now learn the new ways of God, likewise making them habitual by yielding your body to the service of righteousness (vv. 13, 16, 19). But you have not yet fully done so, and to the extent that you are failing, you become vulnerable to sin (and sin's cohorts) by conforming to the ways of the evil one. This is the *war within* that you must wage in order to win the war without. It is, therefore, important to understand something of those ways in order that you may avoid them and learn to replace them with God's righteous ways (cf. Isaiah 55:8ff.). In the chapters to follow we shall take a hard look at what the Bible says about the world of Satan round about us and those viewpoints, attitudes and actions to which we should be alerted.

Chapter Five

WHAT IN THE WORLD IS GOING ON?

Because of its importance to the understanding of Christian living, we shall continue to look at the *p2* world, the world of Satan, organized and pitted against God and His people. In this world there are three entities that seek to drag the Christian down. John calls them "the desire of the flesh, the desire of the eyes and the pride of life" (I John 2:16). Often in Christian circles they are similarly called, "the world, the flesh and the devil." Because there is little under-standing, and sometimes great misunderstanding of these entities with which the Christian must deal, we shall devote this chapter to a discussion of them.

The "world" about which John frequently writes is the *p2* world that was described in the previous chapter. It is the kingdom of Satan existing on this planet at any given time, ruled by him and used by him to hinder the progress of the kingdom of God on earth. It is composed of all who have never been redeemed by the blood of Jesus Christ. It is not nec-essary for them to recognize the fact that they belong to this kingdom, that they serve Satan and his angels and that they oppose God and his kingdom. For the most part, they are blissfully unconscious of the "scattering" in which they engage (cf. Matthew 12:30).[1] That, as a matter of fact, is a large part of what is meant by "the pride of life." They have been lulled into thinking that they are free of all restraints, doing what they want—rather than being ruled by the evil one. His deception, begun in the garden, has continued throughout history. Those who are subject to him believe that they are able to be like God, self-sufficient, autonomous and wise—whereas the opposite is true.

That Satan's subjects are ignorant of the fact that they are members of the kingdom of darkness is to be expected. Ignorance of the truth is characteristic of this kingdom. By the characterization "darkness" Paul *intended* to signify ignorance, as well as sin and death. Satan is the great liar and deceiver (Revelation 12:9). Evidence of this unawareness on the part of the world is clear from the dialog of Christ with the Jews found in John 8. There, the lying protest that they are in bondage to no one (v. 33) is met by Jesus' declaration that they are sin's slave (v. 34), that they are children of Satan who carry out his desires (v. 44) and

---

1. Here, the image is of scattering rather than gathering sheep. It is the picture of negative activity in relationship to Christ's work. Note: *all* who do not gather (as believers do) scatter. Every non-Christian's life is destructive whether or not he knows this fact or intends to do damage to God and His world.

that they are estranged from truth (v. 45). One great fact about the world, then, is its near total[1] unawareness of its allegiance to Satan. That, of course, is a major achievement of the great Deceiver.

But the believer must never be taken in by Satan's deceptions as are his own followers. Yet, all too often, they are. The world is attractive. As the believer looks at it, desires often arise from what he sees ("the desire of the eyes"). Christians are drawn into its activities by these attractions. How often do academics in Christians universities and theological seminaries, for instance, obsequiously seek to measure up to the "standards" of unbelievers! Frequently, for purposes of acceptance and accreditation by the world they will compromise their positions, beliefs and principles. The entire process of becoming chummy with the world in academic circles has, in turn, filtered down to the grass root Christian church through the graduates of these institutions. Worldly ways, beliefs and methods have found fertile soil in the church. This is so true that in some places biblical ways and means are laughed out of court as simplistic by those who ought to rejoice in them. Rather, while claiming to be "professional," they adopt the stan-

---

1. There are those who overtly seek to serve Satan, though they are in the minority, and one wonders whether many of them believe what they assert to be true or whether for ancillary reasons they strike the pose of Satanists.

dards and ways of the world. Thus, too often, Christians may find themselves among those who "scatter" rather than "gather" the sheep. From reading Christ's words in Matthew 12:30 (cited above) one cannot help wondering from time to time whether or not some of those who profess faith, but are so zealous to bring "worldly wisdom" into the church, are truly disciples of Christ. Paul clearly expressed God's negative opinion of "worldly wisdom" in I Corinthians 1 and 2 where he contrasted God's wisdom with it. It is difficult to understand how Christians can align themselves with those who hate Christ and seek to destroy his church. James had strong words about friendship with the world: "So whoever determines to be a friend of the world thereby sets himself up as an enemy of God" (James 4:4). It is a serious matter, not to be minimized. This is something that needs to be recognized by those who walk close to the edge of the cliff.

But it is not merely a matter of the academician and his students following the world, it is also a matter of the everyday man and woman in the pew as well. If acceptance by the world is a prize sought by the teacher and student, it is also too often a concern of the Christian businessman and laborer. Here, on a different level, but no less real, Satan sets his standards for his subjects who expect the Christian to "run with them" (I Peter 4:4) and are "surprised" when he doesn't (today, we are surprised when he does!). When he refuses, he will experience ostracism (or worse) from the world. Yet, his recognition that Christ and Belial have nothing in common (II Corinthians 6:14-18) will also make opportunities for him to evangelize those whom God is drawing to Himself.

That the world is an attraction for the Christian, as it was for Eve, is patent. It is for this very reason that James warns against the adultery involved in claiming to love God while loving the world (James 4:4). To love the world—or even to become too "friendly" with it—is unfaithfulness to God. Throughout the Old Testament, God speaks to His unfaithful people in terms of the lover who has sought another. This figure shows how heinous love of the world is in God's sight.

To love the world is to love the attitudes and the ways found in the subjects of the kingdom of darkness. It is to live as they do with the same goals, values and motivations, all of which are focused on this world alone. It is to live as if there were no Creator to Whom we must submit. It is to live as if there were nothing more than this life ("eat, drink and be merry, since tomorrow we die"—and that, presumably, is the end of it all). It is to lay up treasures here, forgetting that the task of the Christian is to glorify God and, as a result, lay up treasures in heaven. It is for him to go about "at home" in the here-and-now sin-cursed world rather than live as a pilgrim on a journey to his home in the heavenlies. It is to be satisfied with sin and its consequences rather than longing for "a new heaven and a new earth in which righteousness is at home" (II Peter 3:13). For the Christian, happiness here can be found only in the Lord, in His promises and in following His Word; it can never be attained by acclimating one's self to the world. While the enlightened Christian is always savvy about the world in a deeper way than the world itself (having the Scriptures to rely upon for truthful evaluation of it and its ways), he is never to become a part of that which he understands. Indeed, such understanding ought to lead to his disassociation with the world. When it does not, it is usually because he forgets what he has learned in the Bible. D. L. Moody wrote in the fly-leaf of his Bible, "Either this Book will keep me from sin or sin will keep me from this Book." He was right! We might profitably change that sentence to read "Either this Book will keep me from loving the world or love for the world will keep me from this Book." Love of the world is the danger to be avoided at all costs.

Many of the world's ways and many of its people seem attractive to believers. Otherwise, there would be no appeal. Hollywood, perhaps, is the epitome of this sort of attraction. By means of appealing persons, interesting scripts, fantastic effects, the movie and video industries lure unsuspecting Christians into their fold. The world uses these means to indoctrinate believers to its views and ways. And it grows more and more effective as technology improves and its propaganda becomes more and more subtle.

Worship of sports and entertainment in general has become standard fare for the world. Yet there are believers who can recite the name of each player in the NFL and the team on which he plays who cannot list the names of the twelve apostles. There is something wrong with that! What it points out is that these believers have become so entrenched in the world that their interests are there rather than in the things of the Lord. They fail to obey the command found in Colossians 3:1, 2. And it also indicates that they have too thin an acquaintance with the Scriptures and too great an acquaintance with the world. The answer to both problems is greater familiarity with the Word of God and daily willingness to follow it. Their thoughts and ways need altering (cf. Isaiah 55:8). The Word alone can bring them in line with God's thoughts and ways (cf. vv. 10, 11). In the end, the choice is between the Word and the world.

The second opponent of the Christian is the "flesh." The world is external to him, gaining entrance through the various senses. The flesh is the world internalized within the believer. This is what James is referring to when he speaks of the believer "drawn away" by his own "desires." Because believers were once unbelievers who learned the world's ways and because even as believers they are often influenced by the world's viewpoints, Christians have developed within them desires that displease God. These desires are ungodly desires (John calls them "the desires of the flesh"). Christians lust, enjoy spreading gossip, hate others when they don't get their way, envy, and exhibit pride too. If it were not so, there would be far fewer exhortations in the Bible which, then, would consist of far fewer pages!

I do not want to discuss the "flesh" here in depth. I have written extensively about the biblical concept set forth under that term in my book *Winning The War Within*. I shall simply summarize those data here by saying that "flesh," in the specialized sense in which Paul employs the term, does not mean "sinful nature."[1] Nor does it mean "self."[2] As I have shown in the book mentioned above, the word means *the body wrongly habituated*. Here, body includes brain and everything else material. The body is sinfully habituated as its members are presented to sin for its service. After the process of habituation occurs, one's thoughts, attitudes and actions are automatic, unconscious, skillful and comfortable. These four characteristics of habit make it difficult to change. And when you add to the habitual pull of the body the fact that this body learns to crave (desire) these ways, as

---

1. The New International Version is manifestly not translating but rather interpreting when it renders the Greek *sarx* ("flesh") by those words. Translations should, as far as possible, translate and not interpret when it is not necessary.
2. Some, too cleverly, play games with the word "flesh," turning it around and dropping the "h."

James says, you carry about a formidable enemy with you at all times (cf. I Peter 2:11).

But, believer, there is within you a force even more powerful: the Spirit of God. He is the prime source of power and wisdom (as He enables you to understand and follow the Bible) that God has given you to fight against the sinful desires and habits of the body (Galatians 5:16-24). He is more than a match for the flesh, as Romans 8 indicates. Given such a Resource and Power, it is possible for the Christian not only to put off the old ways of the flesh but to incorporate the new ways of God.

The "Devil" is the third entity in the triad that the world sets up against the Christian. Christian living means living in such a way that one recognizes that there is a world, there is the flesh, and there is the devil to contend with. Those who think too little about the devil are likely to fall prey to his lures and his traps. Those who concern themselves too much about him are likely to do the same. Again, it is utterly essential to strike the biblical balance in all things—including this all-important matter.[1] Satan's interest lies neither in one nor in the other extreme. If he can dupe you into thinking he is inconsequential that is fine. A soldier, unaware of the enemy's presence and power, is vulnerable. If he can immobilize

---

1. For more on the problem of maintaining a biblical balance in all things, see my book *Maintaining the Delicate Balance in Christian Living*.

you by fear, that is equally as good. Avoid both extremes. Earlier, I spoke of how the Christian should think of the devil. He is a roaring lion, but limited. A power, but not as great as the Power within the believer. A dangerous, but defeated foe.

The importance of the recognition of these forces arrayed against the Christian cannot be overemphasized. Failure here means failure in every aspect of Christian living.

Chapter Six

IN THE WORLD
BUT NOT OF IT

Either the world will influence you, or you will influence the world. There is no question about it. One way or the other, influence will occur. The word "influence" comes from two words "to flow" and "into." Ideas, values, ways of living will flow in one direction or the other: from others into you or from you into others. That is why the Christian must always be aware of whether he acts as light and salt to the world or whether the world acts as darkness and corruption to him. Being an influencer for Christ, rather than being influenced by the world is not easy. As a matter of fact, it is probably the most difficult task with which the Christian is faced.

That one cannot escape from the world is a given (I Corinthians 5:10^c). Ascetics have tried—and failed miserably. The selfishness and haughtiness of the so-called "contemplative life" is apparent. The mystic seeks and maintains that he has found a direct way to God, apart from the Mediator and the Word. He claims a closeness to God in which he and the divine merge into one. Mysticism is a selfish as well as an arrogant approach to life because the mystic believes his special access to God is the most important thing in life, and while he wallows in it, the world can go hang! There is a self-centered absorption in one's self that few other activities can approximate. Of course, the so-called "Christian mystic" is no more in some special relation to God than the Muslim or the Indian mystic. All have an experience that is similar, but it is of their own manufacturing. They fabricate this experience which, they maintain, is so ethereal and blessed they cannot describe it. In many cases, it seems, the "experience" is nothing more than the state one may find at the end of an extended period of significant sleep loss.

There is such an emphasis on the first great commandment in mysticism that the second is utterly forgotten. At length the mystic, having entered into his esoteric experience, finds it difficult to think of himself as anything but in a class of his own. While he may speak of the experience as humbling, humility does not seem to be his outstanding characteristic. Rather, he is inclined to look upon those who have not entered into such experience as spiritual peons. There is nothing about mysticism in the Bible. It is a movement in many religions that has (wrongly) been incorporated into Christianity. But it does not fit. One cannot escape life by seeking ineffable experiences. No, the Christian must live with the *p2* world, have dealings with those who populate it and learn to exalt Christ in it. Jesus exercised a profound influence on the world.

If that is so, what must be the fundamental stance of the Christian toward the world? It is set forth in the title of this chapter: he is to be *in* the world, but not *of* it. Jesus was "in the world" (John 1:10), but in no way could He be said to have been of it (John 8:23). The stance toward the world Jesus took is to be the stance of the Christian as well (I John 4:5, 6).

What Jesus did, we see, is to influence those in the world; He was never influenced by it. He refused to accept its ways and its viewpoints. He saw Himself in antithesis to such things. The Pharisees hated Him for this very reason. He threatened the *status quo* which they had brought into being and wanted to maintain at all costs—even at the cost of His life. Conscientious Christians also will find themselves in antithesis to the world's ways. While in the world, influencing the world by becoming salt (stemming corruption) and light (pointing to the way of salvation and truth), they will keep themselves apart from the world's influence. That is a hard position to acquire and maintain. First, one must become aware of the power of an evil influence. Then, he must meet it not only with resistance, but with a counter influence that exalts the Lord Jesus.

In doing so, there is always the danger of tipping to one side or the other. Often one becomes so tired and disgusted with the ways of the world he is tempted to remove himself as far as possible from it. Mystics and extreme separatists are examples of this tendency. But then there would be no witness to the world. On the other hand, he can become weary in the battles he fights to maintain integrity; he may finally give up, drifting along the course of least resistance. Both are wrong ways of dealing with the world. The believer is to be there, participating in the activities of life alongside men and women of the world—eating, drinking, buying, selling, working, employing—but doing so *as a Christian should*, not as the world does. Living, as some have mistakenly called it, "redemptively." He cannot redeem, but he can influence. Only Jesus Christ redeems. The believer's task is to influence the world: that is what being salt and light means. And he does so when he lives according to biblical truth and standards.

Let's consider some pointed words from the Scriptures about this matter of influence. In I Timothy 6:20-21 Paul writes:

> Timothy, guard that which was entrusted to you, turning away from the irreligious chatter and contradictions of what is falsely labeled "knowledge," which some have professed by taking poor aim and have missed the target of the faith.

Those are sobering words of warning given to this young pastor. As you ponder them, notice how the possibility of influence hovers over the entire warning. The truth entrusted to Timothy is to be "guarded." One guards something that another might wish to steal from him. He is to "turn away from" the influence of those who "chatter" about matters that "contradict" what he has been taught by the apostle. He is to recognize that there are views that are "falsely labeled 'knowledge'" which are nothing of the sort. And persons who have followed such ways it turns out "have missed the target of the faith," a sad fact that means that they have fallen for the world's propaganda rather than accept the truth that is in Christ. That statement not only presupposes the possibility of an evil influence leading one astray, but makes it clear that it has done so among "some" who have professed, but missed, the target of the faith.

Note, especially, the operative verbs: "guard, turn away from." These are two very important matters for the Christian in the world to consider. First, recognize that a part of the mission of the evil one and his followers is to relieve you of your beliefs. That which was entrusted to Timothy was the gospel and that form of teaching which stems from it. If you forget that this is part of the devil's strategy, you are very likely to fall into situations and relationships in which your faith is either watered down or dissipated. Romantic relationships with unbelievers stand high on the list. How readily one finds himself rationalizing his behavior when his emotions take over! For the same reason, situations in which one stands to make a great deal of money also rate high. Compromise and rationalization are rife in those and similar areas. Whenever he finds himself challenged to deny his faith, the Christian must remember that the enemy is anxious to dispel faith and replace it with vain chatter. He is to *guard* that faith. Guarding is done, as in the temptations of Jesus Christ, by responding to temptation with biblical truth ("It is written . . .").

But that is not all. The weak believer will discover that in many instances the very presence of evil influence is too much for him. Others, too, will recognize times when in such instances, he is to "turn away." In other words, as Paul told Timothy, he was to "flee" evil. The unwary person in Psalm 1 fell into a trap because he failed to do so. First, he *walked* toward those dispensing evil counsel. Then he became so interested that he stopped and *stood* to listen to it. At length, he, himself, was *seated* in the chair of those who teach it! There is a definite progression of evil. Influence usually does not happen all at once. It takes time to prevail; it creeps up incrementally. When one recognizes the possibility, he should cut it off at the pass! The error is to "walk" toward sin (or as in Lot's case, to "pitch his tent toward Sodom," eventually to live in the city and even become an official in it). There is never reason to spend time imbibing the counsel of the ungodly (cf. Psalm 1)—even in small doses. To do so results in sending your arrow far off target.

Paul helps you to recognize that there can be a problem of identification. Influences rarely purport to be what they are—rather, they are usually "falsely labeled." Christians need to become critical (in the good sense of the word) about what the world says and does. False labels are usually quite appealing;

after all, that is their purpose. Satan comes as an "angel of light," not in red tights with a pitchfork and a spade on his tail! There are slogans, for instance, that are used to "sell" knowledge (falsely so-called). One of those is "All truth is God's truth." But who is to say that what one presents to you under that slogan is truth? You must carefully examine the claim by means of the Scriptures. It is equally true that "All error is the devil's error." Keeping the parallel slogan in mind may help you to become more critical of claims that, when properly investigated, do not stand up to scrutiny. Watch out also for the phrase "common grace." There is common evil too!

True Christian living comes from following Philippians 1:10 where you are challenged to "discriminate between things that differ by testing them." Proverbs 14:15 says, "The simple believes every word." No Christian is to be naive. Remember, not all that purports to be knowledge is. After all, sin came into the world through the tree labeled "the knowledge of good and evil." There the label was true, but Satan's interpretation of it was not. Adam and his posterity have learned to experience evil with all of its deleterious effects. The knowledge of it was an experiential knowledge—not a mere intellectual one! Satan's appeal to "knowledge" has not changed. Look out for that which pretends to be "further" or "greater" knowledge than that which is found in the Bible.

But what are the characteristics of "false knowl-edge?" While there may be others, two are mentioned here: *kenophonia* and *antithesis*. The first means "empty talk, chatter;" the second "contradictions, opposing viewpoints."

Consider the first: "chatter." At the bottom, much of what the world has to offer is nothing more than this. When you investigate a claim, it falls apart. When you thoroughly discover the roots of a system of thought it turns out to be based on some of the same tired, old, worn philosophy that was discarded generations ago. Look out for overly fine distinc-tions, for new "discoveries," and the like. When you boil it all down, the tendency is to offer *something more*. Always beware of those who claim to be able to enhance what you have learned from the Bible. There is no more to our faith. You don't need some-thing more; all you need is more of the something that you already have in Christ. This is perhaps the most dangerous appeal today, and more have fallen for it than for anything else. The world is clever enough to say, like good Hindus, "You don't need to abandon your faith; all you need do is add ours as well." Modern "evangelicals" now want to get together with Roman Catholics, Mormons, etc. That cannot be. There is a place to draw the line—at the gospel of Jesus Christ!

The second appeal is more blatant: it is to *some-thing different*. Opposing views are often set forth by the world. Satan's second word to Eve was a contradiction "You won't die." Paul is saying, "stay the course." Don't let any seeming contradictions to what you believe move you from aiming carefully, and thus missing God's target. Many contradictions may seem at first to be logical and true. But upon further examination they fail to convince. When Schuller, for instance, says that the Reformers were wrong about original sin and calls for a new reformation built on the doctrines of self-esteem, you should "turn away" from his notions.

And if you don't think you could miss the target, Paul says, "let me tell you that some have already done so" (I Timothy 6:21). Indeed, you should learn from such examples. That, surely, is why he mentions the fact. But some Christians seem never to learn. They allow themselves to become sucked in by everything that comes down the pike, running from one fad to the next. It is a sad state of affairs. It is a dangerous thing to wander from the faith. Jesus once said that whoever endures to the end will be saved. Going over to the enemy is one evidence of spurious faith is. As John put it, "They went out from us, but they weren't of us; because they would have remained with us if they had been of us. But this happened that it might appear that they all weren't of us" (I John 2:19). Every professed Christian enamored with the ideas of the world who turns aside to them had better reconsider the genuineness of his faith. The message Paul sets forth is that while *in* the world, you are not to be *of* the world. You are to influence men and women to trust Christ, but not to be influenced by them to turn from Him. Either you will "turn away from" the "so-called knowledge" of those who propagate it or you will turn away from the truth.

There is one assurance, however. In the "High Priestly Prayer" of Jesus recorded in John 17, He asked that His disciples be "kept" from the evil one (v. 11). The prayer has wrongly been interpreted (even by evangelicals) as a prayer for unity among believers. That view, spawned by the ecumenicists, is patently wrong. Not only would the prayer have failed, if that were the correct interpretation, but the entire passage would be hard to understand. The prayer is for the *preservation* of the disciples remaining in the world and for those who would believe their message. Jesus was leaving the world (v. 11). He could no longer guard them as He had before. So Jesus asks the Father to do so. The "they may be one" clause in this verse has nothing to do with horizontal but with vertical unity. Jesus is asking that the believer in the world may be as certainly united to Himself as are the Father and the Son. Using that inseparable unity as an analogy, Jesus is asking that none of the true believers may be lost. If a true believer, then, you will not be lost. That is a comforting thought in the light of the previous information that we have been considering about missing the target of the faith. But even though not lost eternally, a Christian, strongly influenced by "knowledge, falsely so-called," will suffer many hardships unnecessarily (cf. Jonah), will lose influence among the lost and may even lose eternal reward (II John 8). The matter of becoming a living influence for Christ, therefore, is of great importance.

Chapter Seven

THIS PASSING WORLD

John, who had more to say directly about the *p2* world than the other apostles, also revealed this important truth: "Now the world is passing away together with its desires, but whoever does God's will remains forever" (I John 2:17). The world's ways, the things the world loves, the practices it approves, are all transient. They do not remain. They are "passing away"—into hell! Only the Christian who lives as he should in the world has permanence. Only his ideas, his works, his concern, his desires, as they approximate those set forth in the Scriptures, remain. Paul put it this way: Christians in the present emergency ought to "use the world like those who abuse it. The shape of things in this world is giving way" (I Corinthians 7:31). In other words, this world is so transient that what you do to it, for it or with it is not the essential thing. What really counts is eternity.

What were John and Paul talking about? On the one hand, stability would give way to persecution (I Corinthians 7); on the other, the world was changed as the gospel would be preached in all the world since "the times of the gentiles" had begun. The *p2* world was being invaded. God was now in the process of taking prisoners for His Son Jesus Christ. His scr-

vants were going into the highways and byways and
compelling the elect to come in. He was establishing
a worldwide kingdom that, in contrast to the passing,
man-made kingdoms of this world, would never pass
away or be given into the hands of another. It is eternal (Daniel 7:14). The shape of the world as people
knew it before Christ came was truly passing away.
Prior to that time, as the hymn puts it, "the world in
darkness lay"; only the Jews (and a few others whose
lives they touched) knew and worshipped the true
God. Now the gospel was going into the *np* and *p1*
worlds to the *p2* world living in them. That was a
radical change.

But it is also true, as John said, that nothing in
this world of evil is lasting. There are fads, times of
peace and war, times when the gospel advances,
times when it is curtailed, waves of persecution followed by waves of (outward) acceptance (cf. Philippians 4:10-13). The church is required to endure and
flourish in them all for the honor of its Lord. In His
providence, God is conducting the course of world
affairs in order to bring about all His intended purposes. But we can never know beforehand what they
are (unless prophecy specifically tells us).

If the apostles were saying anything it is this:
everything about the world is temporary. There is
some reason to believe that *hebel*, the word in Ecclesiastes translated "vanity," ought to be translated
"temporariness." That certainly is not as euphonious
a term, I'll admit, but, when you study Ecclesiastes

carefully, you note the great emphasis throughout upon the transitoriousness of life. Even if "vanity" is the proper meaning of the term in this book (more recent studies have thrown doubt on this), the point of Ecclesiastes is that the "vanity" Solomon has in view is that *nothing one does lasts*! That is also the thrust of the apostles' words.

Heraclitus, the pagan Greek philosopher, had sense enough to see this back in the 5th century BC. He wrote "All is flux." Also attributed to him is the statement that "you never step into the same stream twice." Put in more biblical terms, *everything in a world of sin goes to pot.* Your doctor and the local drug store keep your body together as long as possible, but eventually it goes into the ground. The same is true of your automobile, your house (if not while you are living—eventually it will happen). Even denominations, congregations, seminaries, Christian colleges eventually deteriorate as false doctrine creeps into them like kudzu. All you can do is hold things together for as long as possible. Occasionally a revival of the faith may bring new life for a time, but this is not to be counted on; more frequently, the message is passed on to some new manifestation of God's church for the next era.

If such radical change is to be expected with reference to God's work as it is carried on by His people in this world, what is to be expected of the world apart from the steadying influence of the gospel? If it were not for the preserving qualities of His people as the salt of the earth and the restraints of divinely-ordained government, the world would be an impossible place in which to live. The fact that God sends His rain and sun upon the just and the unjust, rather than the judgments that are truly deserved, also makes life tolerable (and even passingly pleasant). Such mercies ought to bring men to repentance and to trust in His Son, but instead, the majority of men go on living as if God did not exist. They continue as if they will not have to face Him at the end of life. They act as if He will not judge them. It is a shame—but true.

Think of how difficult it is to live in a world in which nothing is permanent. The non-Christian has no certainties. He does not know whether abortion is murder or not. He cannot tell you whether drunkenness is a disease or sin. He hovers on the brink of plunging into the "post-Christian era," as it has been called since the 60s. But, at the same time, he wonders whether he ought not retain some of the country's pre-60s values and ideals. He is in a quandary over everything around him. The technological world is sizzling. Every month the computer equipment he purchased a year ago seems more and more obsolete. Should he sell and buy anew—or upgrade? Does he need all the bells and whistles offered that his dinosaur laptop doesn't have? Or can he get along with what he owns for a time yet? How about recording on CD—after all, isn't that just around the corner at a price he can afford? Should he hold out for that? If the shape of the world was changing in Paul's time—what of today!

What about politics—the seeming savior of our time in the eyes of many (even many Christians)? Is there any hope there? Some of us would vote for a do-nothing congress and a do-nothing president and administration! I'd vote in a snap for those who promise (assuming they would keep the promise) to do nothing but play chess, eat, drink and be merry throughout their terms, but to leave things as they are for 4 to 8 years. Change in tax rules, change in Social Security, change in business policies, etc., etc., make it almost impossible for anyone in business or the home to plan for the future. That, in turn, leads to a society that is oriented only to the present. Present gratification, indeed, is the order of the day. Expect something from an administration that runs on a platform that is discarded and forgotten long before its framers take office, and you will be disappointed. Where is there any permanence? Any security? Any certainty? Any standard that does not change with the next wave of thought? There is none in the *p2* world. Why expect it? The world is in the process of "passing away" (changing). The hymn writer had it right when he declared, "Change and decay all around I see."

But can't Christians with their permanent standard of the Scriptures effect a permanent society? No. Not according to the Bible. Nor do you see this in history. Take the Dutch, Calvinistic, Kuyperian experiment at Christian government, Christian education and Christian—you name it! Where is it all today? Gone! The Netherlands is one of the most liberal, non-Christian lands in the world, seemingly longing always to be in the forefront of advocating the latest anti-biblical values.

The whole message of Daniel is that since one *p2* world-kingdom passes away and another takes its place, permanence, continuity and truth can be found only in God Who is sovereign over the kingdoms of men and Who puts one ruler down and raises another into prominence. And He brought the rulers of the world kingdoms either by faith or by force to acknowledge the fact. Moreover, each served God's purposes in relation to His people. They existed, not by their own prowess, but by the will of God for His declared purposes. All the "change and decay" around that we see is not pointless—that is the message of Daniel. It all has meaning and purpose— whether we are able to discern what these are in this life or not. Some day, when we see things as they are through eyes from which are removed all scales of nearsightedness and prejudice caused by sin, we shall understand what a marvelous pattern God has been weaving throughout history (see my book *The Grand Demonstration* for the underlying biblical dynamic behind that statement).

So what is a Christian to do when realizing that all is flux? He is to rejoice in it, knowing that the flux serves God's ends. He is to relate to change as no one else can. He doesn't look back to the old days nostalgically, he doesn't flow with the new. Rather, he stands by, acknowledging that all is "passing away," using the world as he can, where he can, according to biblical principles in order to lay up treasures in heaven. Participating in those activities of the world that are consistent with his Christian principles, he lives in the world, but he is not of it. He deals with everyone and everything from his biblical viewpoint. He is correctly critical of all he hears and sees. He adopts nothing that purports to be the world's answer to life's problems. He keeps asserting that the real answers are found in Christ both now—as He enables the believer to deal with change—and throughout eternity, where permanence and change blend in marvelous certainty and security for the first time. In short, Christian living in the world is not living that accepts the present world (God doesn't; why should we?), planting one's feet firmly on it. But it is living almost as if one were operating an interactive TV monitor. He watches as the screen depicts item after item but he only touches those things on the screen that he believes the Bible teaches ought to become a part of his Christian faith and life. To change the figure a bit, he manipulates the screen by his point-and-touch method to so change the course of things (though only in a minor and temporary way, it is true[1]), moving them in a biblical direction. Christian

---

1. He votes for the man who (for a time) he thinks

living in the world is a matter of not being swept away by its influences, not bowing to its demands, but maintaining integrity to God and living preeminently for Him—not for yourself or for the world.

---

will best govern the land; he gives occasionally, as he is able, to causes that promote truth and righteousness (but not to excess—as if they were really going to achieve anything permanent). But preeminently, he witnesses to the lost, seeking to elicit the elect to follow Christ here and hereafter.

Chapter Eight

WHAT IN THE WORLD
ARE YOU DOING?

The Bible doesn't leave us with mere abstractions when it comes to dealing with the people of whom the *p2* world is composed. It is quite explicit. I Peter, for instance, is a handbook for Christians living in difficult circumstances. They must act as if they were resident aliens in this world; that is, at a great disadvantage in so far as their surrounding circumstances are concerned. They will be persecuted, treated badly without cause in the home, by government and by the world in general. What is to be their response? I Peter 4:19, in effect, directs the believer to "trust and obey."[1] He directs the believer to God, Who is in control of all things, working all together for his good (Romans 8:28). One way in which this happens is that God uses adversity to bring him into conformity to the image of God's Son (cf. Romans 8:29, the very next verse which explains it). There is much in I Peter that ought to be digested and under-

---

1. For an in-depth treatment of I Peter, see my book *Trust and Obey*. Moreover, see *The Christian Counselor's Commentary* on I Peter in which I have gone into these matters in some detail.

stood by each believer. That is the reason I have but alluded to it here; it takes careful commentary study that would require too much space here to do justice to all that Peter has said. I cannot strongly enough encourage you to study the book in depth.

But there is one passage to which I would refer you: Romans 12:18. In that verse Paul wrote: "If possible, so far as it depends on you, be at peace with everybody." That is a pivotal verse for dealing with unbelievers.

It is not the Christian's part to throw stones at the world. He describes it honestly, so that he may understand it and deal properly with it; he recognizes its wickedness, but he is not in the world in order to condemn it. According to Romans 12:18, he is to be "at peace with *everybody.*" That includes not only his brothers and sisters in Christ, but everyone in the world with whom he has contact. In I Corinthians 5:12 and 13, Paul explains: "What reason would I have to judge those who are outside? Isn't it those who are inside that you are to judge? God will judge those who are outside." What he is saying is that dealing with the *p2* world in judgment is God's business; the Christian has enough to do keeping himself and his fellow believers in line with God's Word.

Christians must realize that "those who are in the flesh *cannot* please God (Romans 8:8). Even if they wanted to (which they don't), they would not have the capacity to do so. We read that God's love (that which He accepts because He gives it) is "poured into our hearts" when the Holy Spirit is "given to us" (Romans 5:5). That means that the non-Christian is capable of fulfilling neither of the two great commandments—to love God and love one's neighbor—since he is devoid of God's Spirit. Love among unbelievers is not the same as love among those who know Jesus Christ. The unbeliever's love is self-generated and, at best, is horizontal (self and others alone are in view). When properly manifested, the believer's love is Spirit-generated and has a strong vertical dimension. So, while deploring what he sees and hears in unbelievers, while avoiding the sin in which they are entrapped, the believer is not surprised to find that people of the world lead lives that are characterized by rebellion against God. Why should he expect an unbeliever to act like a believer? He isn't one. It is hard enough to get believers to act like believers!

So the Christian doesn't throw stones at unbelievers. Too many Christians have become involved in such stone throwing. It is not only a waste of time, but it is forbidden by what we have already seen in the verses quoted above. Moreover, there is too much to do to fulfill the active role in which Paul says the believer ought to engage—attempting to live at peace with unbelievers. To throw stones at one with whom you ought to be cultivating peace is totally inconsistent behavior.

How does one pursue peace with unbelievers? All of what Paul says in Romans 12:14-21 concerns peacemaking. He blesses those who persecute him (v. 14). That means he speaks good and helpful things to him rather than retaliate. His words are carefully chosen, seasoned with salt and calculated to help rather than condemn. The greatest blessing that one can give another is to tell him about the Lord Jesus Christ and what He has done for guilty sinners and call his persecutor to repentance and faith. That, however, must not be done arrogantly. It must be done in love and with compassion—not looking down on him. And it should be done at an appropriate time (remember Proverbs 27:14). Good, done inappropriately, turns into an evil.

Moreover, he is to show empathy with the unbeliever (v. 15). Empathy is deeper than sympathy. He is to enter into his situation even more fully than the unbeliever himself can. He is to look at it from God's viewpoint as this is set forth in the Bible. Empathy is not merely saying that you rejoice or are sorry; it means really rejoicing, really weeping with him. No Cheshire cat grins or crocodile tears are acceptable.

The believer is to find as many ways of living in harmony with the unbeliever as the Bible permits (v. 16). He is to be willing to associate with those who have little as well as those who have much. He is never to think of himself as "above" them. After all, he is no better than the worst sinner he knows. He is a sinner who, but for the grace of God, could have been an even worse sinner.

He is never to avenge himself by returning evil for evil (vv. 17, 19). Instead, he is to do good in exchange for the evil done to him. That is hard, but makes for peace. He leaves vengeance to God, Who has declared that "It is Mine." He makes no attempt to trespass on God's territory. Instead, he makes room for God to move in at the time and place and way in which He pleases. In doing good, two things are pointed out: 1) "plan ahead to do what is fine in the eyes of everybody" (v. 17^b) and 2) heap burning coals on his head by meeting some need that he has (if hungry—feed; if thirsty—give drink; v. 20).

To do anything well (the word here has the idea of doing it with finesse), takes forethought and preparation. Anyone wishing to serve a fine meal knows this. In the same way one ought to give time and energy to the consideration of how to respond to evil with good. The good that one does ought to be extraordinary; it ought to commend itself to *anyone* who might be aware of it ("fine in the eyes of every one"). All of which leads us back to verse 18.

There are two important qualifications Paul adds to the command to be at peace with everybody (not only believers): 1) "If possible" and 2) "so far as it depends on you." Paul is a realist. He isn't interested in mouthing platitudes or giving pious exhortations that are impossible to fulfill. Too many preachers are like that. Those, for instance, who exhort believers to yield completely to God ("If you don't yield it all, you don't yield at all") foster discouragement and despair because they fail to qualify by saying "though perfection is the goal, you won't reach it in this life." Paul isn't like that. These qualifications of the command recognize that you may not be able to fulfill it.

First, it may not be possible to do so. The unbeliever may not permit you to live at peace with him. He may be bent on destroying any such relationship. He may have a penchant for trouble-making. He may be a crusader against all that you hold dear. Well, you must do all you can to be at peace with him, including all the things that I have mentioned in the verses surrounding verse 18. But he may reject the good you do, the empathy you show, the kindness and thoughtfulness that you extend. You have no control over his response. All you can control is yours. You are to do as Paul commands *whether he rejects or accepts your overtures*. Ultimately what he does in response (or what you think he may do) is irrelevant. You are obeying the Word of God.

Second, you are to be sure that you have done *all* that you are supposed to do from your side of the relationship. You cannot control his response, but you are responsible to do your part toward assuring peace. If there is no peace, with a good conscience before God you ought to be able to say, "Well, it isn't because I haven't done all God required of me to bring it about." If there is no peace, it must always be because the unbeliever will not have it. But even then, notice, there is the possibility of breaking through cursing, persecution, evil doing and the like to bring about peace. Heaping coals of fire on his head means to subdue him with kindness. If you are a soldier defending a mountain pass and can shovel hot coals of charcoal (as indicated here, this is smokeless fuel) on the heads of your unsuspecting enemy beneath, what is the result? You have conquered him. He is no longer an enemy. You have effectively put an end to his evil machinations. By the return of good for evil, you are to do this even to persecutors. So you must not give up too soon if there is no immediate favorable response. You are to keep at it until it is obviously impossible to do more.[1] That point will not be reached until you have "heaped coals" on him!

Peace means different things to different people in different circumstances. To the believer it means peace with God, so that all hostility is gone (Romans 5:1). It then means peace from God—an easy confidence in Him that comes from greater and greater trust (Philippians 4), and it can mean prosperity and comfort ("every man under his own vine and fig tree"). Peace with unbelievers will probably be largely on the level of the cessation or prevention of hostilities. Perhaps, in some cases, it will mean a

---

1. The possibilities for peace are so much greater with believers. They have the Word as a common Standard, the indwelling Spirit as a common Enlightener and Empowerer, and the tool of church discipline which is absent from the relationship of a believer and unbeliever.

fairly good relationship, but never one that approximates that which may exist between two believers.

The goal of all of this is to "conquer evil by means of good." But in doing so, one must be sure not to be "conquered by evil" (Romans 12:21). There is always the danger of becoming involved with unbelievers in the wrong ways. While I do not want to repeat what I have said about influence flowing one way or another, it is true; it does. In the pursuit of the kinds of things set forth in Romans 12:14 and following, you have a plan for influencing the unbeliever for Christ. Yet, in trying to do good, one may be caught up in the evil himself (cf. Galatians 6:1[b]). And of course, it should go without saying, that the peace you seek ought not to be a peace at any cost. No compromise of your beliefs may be made—nor need be. When Paul speaks of "becoming all things to all men," he is not talking about accommodating his beliefs or practices to unbelievers to "win" them. He is talking, rather, about accommodating his own personal interests.

How then does the believer live with unbelievers? In peace. His ideal is set forth in Titus 2:14; 3:8; 3:14. Take time to study these verses; carefully interpreted and translated into life and ministry, they amplify the verses in Romans 12 and look at the things from a slightly different perspective that bring peace.

Chapter Nine

WORLD WAR III

I won't vouch for the number III in the title of this chapter; perhaps we're talking about III, IV, V— or who knows how many there may be. But one way or another, you are involved in war with the *p2* world. As a matter of fact, this is an ongoing, continuous world war *because* it involves the world and the Christian. I have alluded to this warfare briefly in a previous chapter. And in that place I made it clear that God expects you to win battles—not to go down defeated. In Chapter Eight, which you have just finished reading, assuming you read in sequence (not everyone does), we saw how Paul said, "Don't be overcome (conquered) by evil but overcome evil by means of good." In that verse, and the one that speaks of heaping charcoal on the head of your enemy, he was referring to the war about which I am writing.

The word for "overcome" ("have the victory over" or "conquer") is *nikao*, which has to do with winning battles. One comes off the winner (conqueror after the "victory" = *nike*; compare the athletic shoe by that name). While the term is used in other contexts and not only about winning a war, as John prominently uses it with reference to the "world," it always has to do with winning battles (or the ultimate battle). Consider a few instances: Revelation 11:7, "the beast . . . will make war with them, and *overcome* them and kill them;" Revelation 13:7, "to make war with the saints and to *overcome* them;" Revelation 17:14 "These will wage war against the Lamb, and the Lamb will *overcome* them."

So, according to Romans 12:21, you are to *win battles* with evil as it is manifested in the lives of unbelievers. That is God's command to you. The peace you pursue (in Chapter Eight we saw that was the goal) is a peace that often (if not always) grows out of hostilities. It is like the US making peace with Germany and Japan after WWII.

Is it realistic to think that this may happen? Will you *really* win battles with evil? God never commands His children to do anything that is impossible. Whenever you come across a command in the Bible, your hopes should rise. You ought to say to yourself, "Here is a possibility for growth." Whenever God commands something, He always provides His children with both the biblical knowledge about what to do and how to do it as well as the Spiritual power to accomplish it. Moreover, you have John's word for it that it *is* possible to "overcome the world." Not only did Jesus say, "I *have overcome* the world" (cf. John 16:33), but later, John wrote to Christians, "you *have overcome* the evil one" (I John 2:13, 14). If it was possible then, it is also possible now.

Of what does this victory (overcoming) consist and how does one bring it about? Obviously, the entire Bible tells you how to live in such a way that you may overcome evil (and the evil one and his hosts) and win victories for Christ. Obedience to biblical commands, following the thinking and lifestyle set forth in the Scriptures and emulating the Lord Jesus (who overcame) will bring victories. But is there anything specifically connected to overcoming the "world?" Yes, indeed, there is.

John, who wrote most extensively about overcoming and about overcoming the world, specifically had these things to say:

1. "I have written to you, young men, because you are strong, and the word of God remains in you, and you have overcome the evil one" I John 2:14. Here, we see that the strength of youth in the service of God's Word is what brought about victory.

2. "Whatever is born of God overcomes the world, and this is the victory that has overcome the world—our faith" (I John 5:4). Here, saving and living faith that grows out of regeneration is set forth as that which brings victory. Obviously, an unregenerate person, as part of the world, cannot overcome; nor would he want to. But the faith mentioned here is not only that initial faith that brings salvation, it is also that abiding and growing faith that enables the Christian to continue through persecution, trial and even death to overcome the world.

3. "You are from God, little children, and have overcome them, because greater is He Who is in

you than he who is in the world" (I John 4:4). Plainly, the Christian has a powerful Ally in the indwelling Spirit, Who is greater than all the resources that the enemy has to throw into the battle. He sets forth the winning strategies in the Word that He inspired; He enlightens believers to understand them (I John 2:20); and He empowers them to be able to follow His instructions. What a strong incentive to take on the enemy whenever he approaches for battle!

4. "And they overcame him because of the blood of the Lamb and because of the word of their testimony, and did not love their life even to death" (Revelation 12:11). Speaking of Christian martyrs and confessors during persecution, this verse says that their unwavering trust in Christ's death for salvation, their steadfast testimony to Him under the most extreme pressure to recant and their willingness to die for Him, if need be, was what brought the victory.

These four verses are pivotal. A careful study of them will convince any dedicated Christian that victory does not come easily. But on the other hand, they should also cheer him (cf. John 16:33), knowing that Jesus' own victory should inspire him to victory as well. The verses are concrete. For instance, the strength of youth is to be employed in battles. It is not the middle aged generals who are out on the battlefield, but those who have the physical stamina of youth. Not frequently enough do we employ Christian youth in those activities that make it possible to

fight battles that involve the entire community of
faith. Yet, frequently, that is precisely what is needed.
The enthusiasm and strength of youth will carry them
on when others, worn by previous battles, will find
their strength flagging. Look at the youthful team that
traveled with Paul. Clearly, he could have done little
that he did with a cadre of old men, afflicted with
gout, arthritis, etc.! The very tiring and difficult task
of travel in those days demanded the strength of
youth. We have to learn in the church to be able to
blend the wisdom of age with the enthusiasm and
strength of youth. That blend, dedicated to serving
Christ, is unconquerable! Too often we divide youth
from age in our churches. We must learn, as John
indicated in the passages we are looking at, to see the
advantages to be gained by the mix of the two.

Weak faith will not win battles. Weak faith tends
to focus one's attention on self. For instance, I have
worked with those who think that they can be lost
again after they are saved. Again and again, they
spend time, thought and energy on trying to discover
how to "keep" themselves saved. It is impossible for
them to do so; therefore, the quest is unending. Only
Christ can keep us. And that is what He does. He
prayed that we be kept (see earlier comments on John
17), he promises to keep (see I Peter 1:3-5) and He
does, in fact, do so (Philippians 1:6). When John
speaks of the victory being "our faith," he refers not
only to the initial faith that justifies, but to that con-
tinuing faith that grows to the point where one may

face the lions and the gladiators as did the early
Christians without loss of confidence in the Lord.
This same faith is what also sends one forth to do battle at work, with relatives, in various social situations.
It is easy to deny the faith under pressure. Latimer
did at first (though later, he went to his death for the
faith), encouraging his younger companion Ridley to
also "play the man" for Christ as the flames con-
sumed them. Those who want to know how to live in
this world must realize that to do so as a committed
Christian means to live *courageously*. The Lord's
example of courage, and how God raised Him from
the dead because He endured to the end, should be
stimulus enough for all believers (cf. John 16:33). In
the verse just cited, Jesus says "take courage." Why?
Because He has overcome the world. His victory
should inspire all of ours. Moreover, you must do so
because in the midst of tribulation in the world (as He
put it) He wants you to have "peace."

How can one have peace in the midst of great
trial? The verse indicates that His words are the sus-
taining factor: "These things I have spoken to you
that in Me you may have peace. . . ." What did He say
that was so important? This verse comes at the end of
the discourses to the disciples before Christ's death
(John 13-15). It is a frank discussion of what lay
ahead and what they are to do to face it successfully.
A weak, fearful Christian might do nothing better
than to make an in-depth study of those chapters. The

words the Lord spoke to them are words intended to strengthen them; they can strengthen you too.[1]

The fact that the Holy Spirit within you (or among you) is mentioned by John (I John 4:4) ought not to be missed. Everything you do to fight battles with evil in your own wisdom and strength will fail. Indeed, it will amount to aiding and abetting the enemy. There are always two extremes to avoid—asking the Spirit to do what you are commanded to do, instead of doing it yourself and, on the other hand, trying to do it all by yourself. Both are wrong. Many err by leaning only one way or the other. The biblical center in this matter is plain: *You* must obey, but by the wisdom and the power of the *Spirit*. There is no either/or in this matter but a both/and.

In this regard, the words of the elders should encourage: "Stop weeping; look, the Lion that is from the tribe of Judah, the Root of David, has overcome" (Revelation 5:5). Because He has overcome, He is able to open the book of judgment and right all wrongs. That is important. Inequity is the order of the

---

1. The *Christian Counselor's Commentary* on John is one aid to help you do so. But for a serious study of these chapters you will need eight or ten commentaries to accomplish it. If you are a Christian who cares to serve well, you will probably begin stocking your personal library with various biblical commentaries and reference books—and will use them regularly.

day right now—regardless of the social manipulators who attempt to fix the problem (only to mess things up even more). But some day all will be reversed. There is a judgment when He Who is Judge of all the earth will do right. So in times when you want to retaliate (and thereby lose the battle; cf. Romans 12 once again), read II Thessalonians 1:5-12 and take heart. God will turn the tables.[1]

And when all is said and done, the overcomer has this wonderful promise: "He who overcomes, I will grant him to sit down with Me on My throne, as I also overcame and sat down with My Father on His throne" (Revelation 3:21). That statement alone must have strengthened many of the martyrs to stand up to the soldiers of Rome and to the wild beasts of the coliseum to endure to the end. Should it not also encourage you—whose life is *not* on the line—in Christian living?

---

1. An expression, I understand, that comes from turning around a game table to face the opposite direction so that the one who is winning in chess, checkers, etc., will change.

Chapter Ten

THE WORLD'S FARE

The world is caught in the morass of falsehood. But it does not know it. Indeed, many of the world's leaders in every field—politics, education, religion—are avid proponents of one or another of the many forms of falsehood. In this chapter, we will take a look at how the world attempts to influence the Christian by infiltration of its religious ideas into his thinking and his church. The devil must rejoice in the religious confusion that abounds in Christianity today!

Once more, we turn principally to John. In his first epistle he urges, "don't believe every spirit, but test the spirits to discover whether they are of God, because many false prophets have gone out into the world" (I John 4:1). In a day in which more cultic ideas are abroad that ever before, the exhortation is timely. But what is he talking about, and how does one go about obeying this exhortation to test those spirits in the world?

Christian, you cannot believe everyone who claims that he has the Spirit. Many make the claim falsely today, as they did in New Testament times. In I John 2:19, he explains that these false prophets "went out from among us, but they weren't of us;

because if they had been of us, they would have remained with us. But this happened that it might appear that they all aren't of us." There is a lot in that sentence. Schismatic false teachers left the apostles and the churches that they founded in the early days, claiming they had truth "beyond" that which the apostles taught (II John 9). They were in error, but to many they sounded plausible or there would be no such warning given. Moreover, the problem was one anticipated by Christ and the disciples, who warned against it (cf. I Timothy 4:1; Matthew 24:11; Acts 20:29, 30; II Peter 2:1; Jude 17, 18). This, then, is important for the Christian, bombarded on every side by a multitude of views, to grasp. The world is actively propagating error about the Bible, about Christ, about the way of salvation. And you are commanded to "test the spirits." The word for "test" used by John was used for testing metals to see if they would ring true. It has in it the idea of proving or disproving the claims made. You may get help from your pastor and elders, but each one of you is personally responsible; learn to apply the biblical test to claims made about God's truth.

"How am I to do so?" you ask. That important question is answered in the passage we are looking at in I John 4. He is calling these false prophets the mouthpieces of evil spirits. By testing their claims, you test the spirits. He doesn't have any idea of putting you in contact with demons. Never is that taught in the Bible. John's meaning is explained by the use of a specific example. In verses 2 and 3 he says, "By this you know God's Spirit: every spirit that confesses that Jesus Christ has come in the flesh is from God, and every spirit that doesn't confess Jesus isn't from God." There is the test illustrated by a current example of the prevalent error of that day—gnosticism. Gnosticism taught that the flesh was evil and that the Christ came on the man Jesus at His baptism, but left before His crucifixion. In another form, it taught that the body of Christ was not real; it was only a phantom body. In both forms, there was a denial of the fleshly (bodily) coming and death of Jesus Christ. This was heresy. The test is conducted by asking, WHAT DOES THE PROPHET TEACH? If they taught He came bodily, they were of God; if they denied it they were not.

"But," you say, "If you check out their doctrine of the incarnation, Roman Catholics and Jehovah's Witnesses believe in the bodily coming of Christ. How is it a test of orthodoxy to ask whether one believes in Christ's bodily coming?"

You are asking a good question. Many think that the test is to ask about the incarnation. In one convoluted manner or another, they attempt to apply this to all cults and false religions. That is the wrong approach and, assuredly, is not what John taught you to do. Remember, I said John gave you a specific example of the test. Gnosticism, largely of a Cerenthian sort, was rife in the region John served. It was natural, since much of his book is concerned with refuting Gnosticism, that John would take the prominent example of false teaching plaguing his readers as that example. But it was only one example of the basic test. The test is, remember, *What does the prophet teach*?

That is the general test into which this example fits as one instance. Note especially in this regard how the test itself is stated in verse 6: "We are of God; whoever knows God listens to us, but whoever isn't of God doesn't listen to us. *From this [test] we know the spirit of truth and the spirit of error.*" Do you see? The test is to discover whether the teaching accords with the teaching of the apostles.

Today, of course, we cannot go to an apostle and ask him about a particular teaching. But we can find out what he thought about it from his writings. The apostolic message is recorded in the pages of the New Testament.

Notice John's argument. You have not been led astray by their errors because the Holy Spirit in you is greater than the evil spirit in the false prophets (v. 4). They speak the wisdom of the world and of the one who is in the world, and the world listens to them (v. 5). But genuine Christians *listen to the apostles* (v. 6). In short, the argument is this: birds of a feather flock together.

How then does this work? The test is not to judge by feelings, how "nice" the preacher seems to be, the size of his following, or experience (either yours or another's). The only safe guide is the Bible. All else is fallible. Claims and experiences mean nothing so far as the test is concerned. One judges by the *doctrine* that is preached; nothing else.

The problem is not a new one. It was already a difficulty anticipated in the Old Testament law. In Deuteronomy 13:1-3, we are told that if a prophet or dreamer of dreams prophecies and his prophecy comes to pass, you must not follow him if, at the same time, he teaches doctrine that is out of accord with biblical *teaching* about God and His ways. Moses goes on to say, if he produces a "miracle," he is not to be followed if his *teaching* is astray. So-called miracles are not ever adequate proof of a teacher's claims (cf. II Thessalonians 2:9-11). Moses, himself, was up against false miracles performed by the magicians and priests of Egypt. He understood!

Apropos to this discussion is the great word of Isaiah: "To the law and to the testimony! Whoever will not speak according to this word, there shall surely be no dawn for him" (Isaiah 8:20). The word of God is sufficient. Nothing must be added to it and nothing must be taken from it. Additional prophecies, either verbal or written, are forbidden under serious penalties (Revelation 22:18, 19). It is because christians want something more or something different, as we saw in the section on worldly influence, that they often go for false teachings. One of the major reasons that they hunger for more is because they have so little. Not that there is little in the Bible, but that there is so little of the Bible in them. They do not study the

Scriptures in a serious fashion. The Spirit God gave you does not need to impart truth to you that He has already given to you in the Bible! He will enlighten you to the meaning and application of the Scriptures when you are willing to spend the time prayerfully digging deeply into their meaning.

Because a woman sat on a tripod over a hole from which smoke poured forth in Delphi, and uttered ambiguous prophecies in iambic pentameter, many followed her teaching and the religion that supported it. But though there are no such oracular holes active today (so far as I know), don't for a moment think that if there were there would be no Christians tempted to "listen" to her rather than to Christ's apostles. That's why I John 4 was written. Don't let it happen to you. Test the spirits to see if they are from God!

Chapter Eleven

WHAT IN THE WORLD
IS HE WAITING FOR?

Why has God been waiting so long to wrap things up? Why does He wait generation after generation while men and women defy Him by their thoughts, words and deeds? Why doesn't He send Jesus in flaming fire taking vengeance on the *p2* world, as He has said He will (II Thessalonians 1)? Why does He wait, all the time giving the skeptics and scorners opportunity to jeer and rail against His promise (II Peter 3:3, 4)?

Peter tells us why, Christian. It is so that you could be saved! You—and all those who down through the ages have been "ordained to eternal life" (Acts 13:48). You see, there are two kinds of people out there in the *p2* world. There are some of every generation who will eventually believe the gospel and, like you, desert the kingdom of darkness for the kingdom of God's dear Son. Then, there are those who will go on throughout their lives into eternity in the kingdom of darkness as servants of sin and Satan. They will never savingly believe.

Peter explains to us that God is not slack concerning His promise to come and bring the present order of things with which He is so displeased to an end. Rather, he says, "He is patiently waiting for you, not wanting any [of you] to be destroyed, but everyone to come to repentance" (II Peter 3:9). That is a profound truth. God is putting up with a rebellious world, led by a rebellious angel, in order to graciously gather a people for Himself from many different lands and times.

But why wait so long? For God it is not so long: "one day with the Lord is like a thousand years, and a thousand years are like one day" (II Peter 3:8). And it is interesting to note that Peter went on to say that Christians could "hasten the coming of God's Day" (v. 12). How, in His providence, can that happen? How has He allowed us to participate in moving things forward?

I am not sure of all that Peter had in mind, but this chapter deals with at least one way in which that hastening of His Day can happen. Since God has given to believers the task of bringing people to salvation through Christ by proclaiming the gospel to them, we can become more zealous about the task. Winning the elect to Christ is going too slowly. But, as each one who believes is brought into the kingdom, we should think, "Wonderful, we are one soul nearer to the coming of Christ and the remaking of all things," and enthusiastically throw ourselves all the more into the task.

One of the reasons the work lags is that the whole church is not involved as it should be. The work of winning people to Christ is not the work only of the leaders of the flock; it is the work of every Christian. It is not shepherds who make more sheep, but the sheep themselves. In the early church *everyone evangelized everywhere*: "those who were scattered abroad went everywhere announcing the message of good news" (Acts 8:4). And, in particular, note that this is talking about ordinary Christians (the apostles were not part of this group): "everybody was scattered throughout the regions of Judea and Samaria *except the apostles*" (v. 1). The church had been given marching orders by the Lord (Acts 1:8) but was still bottled up in Jerusalem. So, through the persecutions of Saul (later to become the apostle Paul), God *drove* them into the second stage of their missionary activity. Sometimes, when the church fails to put forth enough effort to proclaim Christ, God uses this method to motivate the church to spread His Word. Let's hope He doesn't find it necessary to do so in our day among our church!

Well, then, how is the message of salvation to be brought to the world? Since there are two kinds of people in the world, we must first recognize that fact. When we do so, we will preach to all since we don't know who is, and who among the people of the world isn't, a part of the elect company who will believe. Just as when someone runs a powerful electromagnet across a mixture of sawdust and iron filings, and the iron filings jump out and adhere to the magnet, so too, as the gospel is preached to all, the elect believe.

To know that there is an elect group among the *p2* population is encouraging to evangelism. There are those who *will* respond to the gospel. There is no doubt about it. Your efforts will not be in vain. The task is to present the way of life to as many as possible in as short a time as possible in order to hasten the day when there are no more left to come to Christ.

What is the message? It is a message of repentance and faith (Acts 20:21). But what is repentance, and what is faith? The Greek word for repentance means "an afterthought; a rethinking so as to have a change of mind." There is no repentance apart from a person's recognizing that what he thought, when a servant of sin and Satan, was wrong. He must come to see that God is not a pushover Who doesn't care about sin. Instead, he must realize that He is holy and demands holiness of us. He must recognize that he is a sinner who has broken God's holy law and stands condemned to eternal damnation. He must change his ideas about Christ as a great man and recognize Him as the God-man Who came to die on the cross, bearing the sins of all who would believe in Him. These matters demand a radical change of thought.

But repentance is inseparably connected with faith. Realizing these things, this person will trust in what Christ did on the cross for his salvation, believing that Jesus died in his place, bearing the guilt and its penalty for him. This faith is a trusting that depends wholly on what Jesus did rather on anything he can do.

The Old Testament word for repentance completes the picture. It means "turn about." If the person's change of mind is genuine and his trust is true, he will want to live henceforth for the Lord out of gratitude and love. This turning is from Satan to God, from sin to righteousness, and it is brought about by the Holy Spirit Who, through regeneration, has come into his heart (Romans 5:5). It is God who "quickens" or "gives" [spiritual] life to believe (Ephesians 2:1ff.). Men do not turn to God on their own. They must be transformed by God Himself to do so. All *should* believe when they hear the gospel, "that Christ died for our sins according to the Scriptures, and that He was buried, and rose again from the dead according to the Scriptures" (I Corinthians 15:3, 4)—but only the elect *will*. The two facts of Christ's death and resurrection constitute the "good news." There is no good news about the death of Christ alone. A dead savior is no Savior. The good news must also include His resurrection from the dead.

Remember, Christ actually died for the sins of the elect. He suffered in their place. There is no possibility of any of the elect not being saved. They could never pay the penalty for their sins in hell if Jesus has already done so. Jesus didn't come merely to make salvation possible; He came to save. What He did on the cross is not frustrated by man's unbelief, as some teach; His death was for His own and is effective: "Everybody that the Father gives Me will come to Me, and whoever comes to Me I certainly won't cast outside" (John 6:37; see also v. 39).

How does one present the gospel? There is no one way. Indeed, as we see Jesus Himself dealing with individuals, we see variety in approach. The message is the same ("Believe in Me as the Savior"), but the way in which it is delivered never seems to be the same. In John 3, for instance, Jesus confronts Nicodemus straightforwardly: "You must be born again." In the very next chapter, He slowly leads the woman at the well to faith, talking first about water and wells, buckets and husbands until she finally sees that He is not merely a teacher or prophet but the Messiah Himself. In chapter 9, Jesus heals the blind man, but says nothing about eternal life. It is only later on that He confronts him about the need to see spiritually. Variety of approach, growing out of the situation at hand, seems to be the method He used. That method cannot be improved upon today.

While you save no one (God alone does that), He expects you to present the message attractively (Titus 2:10), persuasively (Acts 18:4), prayerfully and clearly (Colossians 4:3, 4), and then leave the rest to Him.

Chapter Twelve

WORLD CLASS CITIZENS

"Class," in the sense of living a high toned lifestyle, is what we ought to find among Christians. That is to say, they ought to approve of and follow after the better things of life—the highest sort of art, music, literature, manners, style, speech, etc. That is *not* to say that they must belong to the upper class of citizens as the world recognizes wealth and culture, but that they ought to strive to align themselves with those things that excel. How do we come to this conclusion? The passage in Philippians 4:8, 9 indicates as much:

> Finally brothers, whatever is true, whatever is serious, whatever is just, whatever is pure, whatever is lovely, whatever is of good repute, if there is anything morally excellent and if there is anything praiseworthy, focus your thinking on these things.

In this place, Paul uses words that, without exception, call for the highest sort of living. They are words opposed to all that is sordid, low, crass, false and tawdry. Let's examine the categories of things in this important list.

But first, understand the context. In Philippians 3:20, Paul had spoken about our citizenship being in heaven. Rome established colonies, of which Philippi was one. In these colonies, the residents possessed dual citizenship—that of the local city (Philippi, in this case) as well as Rome (a very valuable citizenship, with great privileges). Paul saw Christians in much the same boat. Christians too possess dual citizenship. But Philippian citizens had responsibilities and opportunities in Philippi; they weren't concerned only with their Roman citizenship. So, too, the Christian has to live in the world here, even though he possesses heavenly citizenship which is far better. While still living here, he must deal with the things around him wherever he lives, making choices about what occupies his mind. This list of categories helps circumscribe the territory that is legitimate for the Christian. Instead of worrying, for instance, he is to busy his mind with the sorts of things that fit these categories.

The first mentioned is "whatever is **true**." This probably doesn't exclude fiction or imagination except when it is palmed off as if it were truth. We live in a phony society. The world lives largely in pretense. Christians are not to do so. They are not to be one thing to one person and the opposite to another, deceiving both. They are to think about those things that constitute the facts of the world around them. The Christian doesn't live in hopes of impossibilities. He doesn't dream of things that could never be. He knows basic facts about God, man, creation, the future, and so on. His thinking is to be contained within the parameters of those certainties. He is

Bible-oriented and, therefore, truth-oriented. He does not flit from one falsehood to another, hoping somewhere, someday to find truth; he possesses it in Christ. In John 18:37, Jesus made it clear that He came to "bear witness to the truth." His kingdom, "which is not from here," is a kingdom based on truth. It is not like others which have no such firm foundation. Everything about this "kingdom of light" (a metaphor for truth) reflects truth. Naturally, then, he will be sure that those things in the world around him, with which his thinking is concerned, are based on truth. Hollywood films, for instance, for the most part, despite all the pretensions made about them, are not likely to be true to life. They stress the sensational and often teach what the producer wants life to become.

"Whatsoever is **serious**" is the second item on Paul's list. The word *semnos* is a large term, meaning "honorable, venerable, dignified." It has to do with things that have stood the test of time and are worthy of remaining. It is opposed to faddism. In Greek usage, it is a word frequently used to describe the dignity of the gods. Christians, then, are to choose their concerns from among the tested virtues of life. They are not to be deceived into following the latest trends, buying into things that have not been considered long enough to know how they will turn out. Instead, many Christians (and Christian churches), trying to be "up to date," get themselves suckered into all sorts of things that, later, they regret. Christians should give careful consideration before abandoning the old, tried and true ways. That doesn't mean they will give up on progress (especially in technological areas), but it does mean they will not be too quick to snap up everything that comes along. Much Church Growth thinking is not *semnos*.

The third item on Paul's list is "**just**." It has to do with that which is right, upright, fair, impartial. When the Christian is forced into taking sides, he is to end up, every time, on the side of that which is right. He is never to side with evil. He may often find that neither side is in the right—and must say so. But insofar as it is possible, he always ends up on the side of that which he believes to be fair, just, right. He cannot give any other sort of counsel. While he is as wise as a serpent, he is also as harmless as a dove. His craftiness is always in the service of that which is true, fair and just. He cannot testify against his neighbor in any other way than that which he believes to be factual. He knows and reckons with his own biases. His thinking is always along the lines of what is fair, just, right. He trains his mind not to think in devious but in straight ways. He works at keeping his thinking in check.

The next item on Paul's list is "**pure**." This word, meaning chaste, sincere, originally meant "being prepared for worship" (Souter). It is truly the word for our day. Books, films, videos, advertisements, etc., all seem to feature the opposite. The sordid is the order of the day. It is unnecessary to expatiate on this term since it is clear enough. The problem, in a sex-saturated society, is to be able to keep one's thinking pure. Not to store up impure images, not to give time and thought to such things, means not to indulge one's mind with them in the first place.

The next item on Paul's list is "**lovely**." This is an interesting word. It includes those things that are truly pleasing, acceptable, lovable, gracious, inherently attractive. It rejects all that is superficial—symbolism vs. substance—all that is misleading and all that on the surface looks good, but underneath turns out to be bad. It is a *hapax legomena* (which means that it occurs only once in the New Testament; here). It encompasses all that has beauty in and of itself. It must be sharply distinguished from those things that Satan has made attractive for the wrong purposes. Its attraction is always toward uplifting the life and character of those who are attracted to it.

The final item on Paul's list is "whatever is of **good repute**." It means that which is praiseworthy, noble, high-toned, whatever has the right ring to it (as when clicking a fingernail against fine crystal). It means high class—that which is on the better end of life. This does not mean class in the sense of wealth or prestige, but in the sense of choosing not the good or the better, but the best. Christians, too often in building their church buildings, settle for that which is cheap, that which is second-rate. They ought to do as well as they can with what they have. A shoddy, cinderblock building sitting on a lot that hasn't been mowed since the flood is a disgrace to Christ. Better not to build until one can do so well, and keep the property in good repair, than to throw up any old kind of building and then have the gall to advertise that the Lord's church meets there. Usually, the second-rate nature of things is due not to the lack of funds among the members but to their unwillingness to shell out! They will take every shortcut in the book in order not to do so.

Then, Paul sums up with two other words: "if there is anything **morally excellent**, if there is anything praiseworthy." The first word, "morally excellent" is *arete*, a term very famous in Greek literature meaning "virtuous, of merit, of worth." It meant one's rightness in relationship to the commonwealth. Christians ought to rightly represent the heavenly land of which they are citizens.

The second means "**commendable**." Much is excluded from the Christian's purview. Even the world rejects much that it considers not commendable. If the world puts thumbs down on something as sordid, too rotten for themselves, surely the Christian ought not to be involved in it. Clearly, this whole list tends toward the better side of things. Whatever is in a class that is distinguished from the worst, the sordid, the dishonorable is to be considered by the Christian.

Some things may pass the test of one or more of these items on the list, but not others. Here is where some Christians go wrong. It must pass the test of *all*.

Some, for instance, speak highly of a movie's special effects, plot, the acting abilities of the cast—but the movie fails to pass the test of being "pure, lovely." Because of one they seem to forget the other items. None is to be bypassed in the process of evaluation.

Note, all this has to do with the thought life. The context calls for that. Paul has just talked about not worrying. The worrier, one who concerns himself about things not true ("What if such and such takes place?"), certainly doesn't concentrate his thinking on those things that are lovely, and his thinking is opposite of that which is of good repute. He doesn't pass the thought life test. The principles here, however, have application to matters beyond worry; they pertain to all of life. The end doesn't justify the means: we don't do evil that good might come.

The thought life is also emphasized because this is the place to cut off the action. First a matter is in thought; then in action. I have counseled child molesters who (to a man) will tell you that they thought about it for quite some time before building up enough "courage" to do anything. Often, this involves self-deception where the perpetrator of the crime must "justify" it to himself by a tortured, twisted process of rationalization ("My wife isn't satisfying my needs." "My daughter has been asking for it by the way she dresses and looks at me.").

All in all, this list is a practical, daily guide to decision-making in the world. If you are not sure whether an activity (or the thought of it) is worthy, refrain until you are. The holding principle in Romans 14:23 is clear: "Whatsoever is not of faith is sin." That is to say, even if the thing isn't wrong in itself, but you go ahead and participate in it thinking it is (or might be), you sin. You sin, not because it is wrong, but because *you* are. Your attitude in entering into it was sinful. You thought something like this: "Even if it is sin, I'll do it anyway." Your attitude toward God was sinful. So be careful about how you apply the principles. The very existence of six principles and two summary statements, making eight tests in all, is helpful in approaching an area from several different angles. Don't fail to use each of these. This list, applied and followed carefully, will truly make you a world *class* citizen in God's eyes!

Chapter Thirteen

SUMMARY OF FACTS ABOUT THE *p2* WORLD

There really isn't much more to say about the Christian's relations with the *p2* world. So I wish simply to sum up before going on. It is a world dominated by Satan and his ilk. It is a world opposed to the Christian. It is a world in which there are temptations to follow the world, the flesh and the devil. It is a world in which influence flows all the time—either in the direction of the Christian or the world. It is a world in which the Christian is a fisher of men. He is out to hook all those who have been ordained to eternal life. It is a world in which there are differences; some things are so sordid that the believer may have nothing to do with them. Others fit the categories of Philippians 4:8. Since he must choose which activities he will identify with, his choices are always to approximate those things recommended in this verse.

The world has power. But its power is not overwhelming. It may deceive, tempt, but it may not make the Christian sin. The evil one may not even "touch" the believer. Christians ought, then, to be wary of but ought not to fear the devil and his crowd. They ought to walk circumspectly and make choices according to the Scriptures. When the believer sins, he may never say, "The devil made me do it." He did it himself. He may never blame other Christians or unbelievers for his faithlessness. He is responsible for all his thoughts, words and actions.

The Christian, while a citizen here, is also a citizen of heaven. He must not live as if this were false. Rather, he ought to live above the world's highest attainments. That is to say, his standard, being God's standard, is higher than that of the world. He is to think God's thoughts after Him and follow in His ways (Isaiah 55:8). His lifestyle, as he lives among those who possess only one citizenship, is to be exemplary of the dual citizenship that he has.

The obedient Christian will not become fixed upon the things of this world. He will hold them lightly. But he will use them to the full, realizing that they are here for that purpose. He is careful to transform as many of this world's things into eternal treasures, which he is laying up for the future, as he can. As he wends his way through the course of this life in the world, his eye is fixed on the eternal city and the heavenly inheritance, not the least of which is seeing his Lord face to face.

All in all, if he does not become a world class citizen in the true sense of that phrase, it is entirely his fault. All the resources necessary for this have been provided by God in His Word and by His Spirit. Think deeply about these things before we move on to the last use of the word "world" in the next chapter—the *p3* world.

Chapter Fourteen

THE NEW WORLD ORDER

Many Christians do not realize what momentous events occurred when Jesus Christ came to earth. It was not only a Savior coming to a small group of His people in the land of Palestine, but by that event the *entire world* was affected. Since that time there has been a great shift in the religious situation in the world. Prior to Christ's advent, there was but a very insignificant group of people who knew the true God—largely Hebrews by race (and a few others who lives were savingly touched by them). Now that people, as a whole, rejected Jesus Christ and, consequently, no longer knows the true God. Instead, today, it is among the nations of the world that He is almost exclusively known and worshipped by Gentiles. Since the coming of Jesus, then, we have lived in the "times of the Gentiles."

Paul had a lot to say about this in the latter portions of Romans. There, he described how the natural branches of God's kingdom had been cut off and the wild branches had been grafted in their place in the same olive tree. The natural branches are the Jews, the wild branches the Gentiles, and the tree from which the former were broken off and the later grafted in, the People of God. This kingdom, spoken

of by Jesus in His parables, which was taken away
from one people and given to another, describes the
formation of a new people which was not before a
people. That is also what Peter was talking about in
Acts 15:14. This great shift in the world was the
direct result of the death of Jesus Christ for the
"world," and not for the Jews alone.

When Jesus gave the great commission (Matthew
28:19, 20), He preceded it with the statement "All
authority is given to Me in heaven and in earth."
Based on this fact He said, "Go *therefore*." The fact
that Jesus was now building a kingdom on earth (as
Daniel had predicted), and that "all" the "authority"
that once had been wrested from Adam by Satan had
now been reacquired by Jesus the Mediator, meant
that things in the world had changed significantly.
This is the "time when everything was to be restored"
(Acts 3:21). Satan's frenzied activity now is that of
the defeated ruler of a defunct kingdom that is in
shambles.

Now, it is important to understand the fourth use
of the "world" against that backdrop. I have spoken
of this fourth use of the term as a use in which the
world is distinguished from Jews only. In contrast to
those who had the idea that the Jews alone had salvation sewed up (as they largely did in the Old Testament era), the truth is that Jesus came as the Savior of
the *world* (not merely as the Savior of Jews). The *p3*
use of the word "world," then, means Gentiles as well
as the Jews of the present believing remnant. You can

see this use in I John 2:2, "He Himself is the appeasing sacrifice for our sins, and not ours only, but for those of the whole world."

To whom does the "our sins only" refer? Who is set over against "the whole world?" The latter expression in John is unique. When John emphasizes the word "world" by the addition of the term "whole," (a qualifier not used elsewhere by him) he is making a special point about this "world." The point is he is speaking of all the nations of the world *as over against* some one portion of it. What is the portion that could possibly be set over against the whole?

Obviously, Jesus didn't lay down His life as an appeasing sacrifice for every last woman, man and child who ever lives. If that were true, no one would be punished in hell. God's wrath would be appeased for all of them. No, he is simply saying that Jesus didn't give His life an atonement for only one portion of mankind, but for people out of the entire world. The portion referred to cannot mean Gentile Christians, because they were a part of the "whole world" of which John speaks. No, he must be speaking as a Jew who now says that Jesus is the Savior of the "whole world" in the sense that some from every nation and tribe and people and tongue" would worship the Lamb (Revelation 7:9[b]). Jesus did not come to die for *Jews only*, but for people from all parts of the world. That explanation of the verse alone makes any sense.

When Jesus says in John 3:16 that "God so loved the world," He was referring to this same fact. There was love for people from all parts of the world, not for Jews alone. Clearly, it did not mean every last person because He makes it clear that "whosoever *believes* in Him" will "not perish but have everlasting life." The saving love of Christ was extended throughout the world to some in every part of it who would believe from all peoples of the world. The apostles were to "make disciples from all the nations," because their task was world*wide*. As Paul put it, "God wanted to make known what is the riches of His glory of this secret among the Gentiles, which is Christ in you, the hope of glory" (Colossians 1:27). And in the same chapter, he spoke about the gospel which "in the whole world is bearing fruit" (1:6). Again, the "whole world" emphasis is on the fact that the gospel is for all nations and peoples.

So when the Samaritans declared that Jesus is the "world's Savior" (John 4:42), they may, or may not, have had a full understanding of what the words meant. But at least, they saw clearly that Jesus had come to save others, like themselves, and *not Jews only*. It was what motivated Paul to preach even when his brothers according to the flesh refused to believe (cf. Acts 13:44- 49). The Gentiles heard the Old Testament prophecy of the fact that salvation was to go to "the ends of the earth" and were glad (Acts 13:47, 48). This prophecy was the background for Jesus' command to preach to the "uttermost parts of the earth." There can be no doubt, then, that a fourth use of the world, relates to those in every nation to whom the gospel would be preached in contradistinction to Jews only.

The same idea of non-limitation of people or class is found in a slightly different form in I Timothy 2:1-7. Here we read, that Jesus "gave Himself as a ransom payment for all [sorts of] persons" (v. 6). The words in brackets are not merely added; they are one very possible translation—the most likely one. In fact, we shall see that they actually constitute the right translation of the sentence. In verse 1, Paul calls for prayer for all [sorts of] persons, among whom in verse 2 he includes kings and all in high positions. The idea here is that these prayers should not be limited to any one class. Include even those in authority in government, he urges. Why? Because God wants "all" [sorts of] persons to be saved—i.e., even those in high places (v. 4). All through the passage the "all" should be translated (as it might legitimately be) "all sorts of." This is in contrast to narrow views that think only one class or sort of person is eligible for salvation. No. Some out of every nation, and—it would seem—some out of every class of persons in every nation, were those for whom Jesus died. Again, in Hebrews 2:9, this nonexclusive emphasis comes to the fore: "He suffered death, so that by God's grace He might taste death for all sorts of people."

There is no reason to believe that in ordinary writing the word "all" usually includes every man, woman and child ever born. That, as we saw earlier, happens only on rare occasions. When all of you speak, you use the word "all" in a way that means all of a particular group, class, etc., usually of a group about which you have been speaking [here, I used it to mean *most of you to whom I am writing;* conceivably, there are some reading this who never use it in any but an absolute manner]. The recent quip, spoken in a negative manner, says it all: "Nobody goes there any more; it's too crowded!"

When the seventh angel sounded his trumpet and the mighty voices cried out, "The world's empire has become the empire of our Lord and of His Christ, and He shall rule forever and ever" (Revelation 11:15), they were saying no more than Christ did in the preface to His great commission. Both were affirming that what Daniel had predicted (ch. 2, 7) had actually come to pass. Peter said it in these terms: "Let the whole house of Israel know for certain that God has made this Jesus Whom you crucified both Lord and Christ" (Acts 2:36). Jesus now sits on the throne (Revelation 3:21).

There are many who think that Jesus died for everyone in the absolute sense. That could not be because if He actually bore the penalty for people who are now suffering the same penalty in hell for the very same sins, not only would God be unjust in exacting the same punishment twice, but the death of Christ would have been ineffective and worthless.

Either the death of Jesus atones or it does not. Either it satisfies God for sins or it does not. You can't have it both ways. Indeed, if it doesn't do these things, and only makes salvation available, or possible, then there is no salvation at all. If to make it effective I must contribute something to it, that is the weak point where it must fail. It is all of grace, or there is no sure salvation for anyone. I do not make salvation effective by faith. My faith is non-meritorious. Faith is but the instrument by which I reach out and receive the free gift of salvation (already wrought by Christ on the cross). Either He suffered efficaciously for sins or He suffered in vain.

No, everyone limits salvation. Biblically, the *scope* of salvation is limited to those elect persons, all of whom will believe. Others limit the *power* of salvation. For them it is not complete until men somehow or other add the necessary catalytic ingredient to bring it to pass. The rest of us, together with all of the Reformers, believe that Christ's death on the cross and His perfect obedient life saves all for whom He died. It does the job.

So, there are four ways in which the word "world" is used. The non-personal world, the personal world, including every man, woman and child, the world that lives for Satan and the world as over against Jews only. Keep each in mind as you read the Bible and think about Christian Living in the World. Ask, "Which world?" Ask, "How does it make a difference?"

Chapter Fifteen

CONCLUSION

Until Christ takes him out of it, by death or His return, the Christian must live in the world. Indeed, he lives in the world in all four of its manifestations. While one may be able to distinguish four aspects of the world, he does not live compartmentally. As he lives in the *np* world, he also lives in the *p1*, *p2* and *p3* worlds as well. The *p2* world is not his world in the sense that he no longer lives in communion with it as a part of the kingdom of darkness. In that sense, he no longer lives in it. But in another sense—in the sense that he deals with it all around him, still possesses many of its values and patterns of living himself—he does. These linger on as the "flesh." He may never escape it as long as he is here. He will find it wherever he goes, whether it be to some cave or whether he smothers himself with "Christian" activities. So, concurrently, he lives with and in all four worlds.

In the sense of the last world we studied (the *p3* world), he ought to be thrilled that, though it has not yet reached its fulfillment when all things will be replaced by a new heaven and a new earth in which righteousness is at home God has already set up His kingdom here and is reigning over His church in the midst of this world (which, of course, is none other than the *p2* world in essence) in a worldwide manner. This kingdom is not from this world (neither the *p1* nor the *p2* and *p3* worlds) in the sense of its origin and its direction, otherwise His servants would fight. But this kingdom of truth and of light is nonetheless real. It shall never pass away. It will continue until all things are caught up into it in perfection in the final state of things. It is, you must remember, the triumphant kingdom that is spreading throughout the world. Its King and Head is the Lord Jesus Christ. Christian, you are a part of this wonderful kingdom, the church of Christ. Some day, the world will no longer be fractured as it now is. There will be but one world. Then the Kingdom of God will be coextensive with it. But until that day, as you live before the present divided world, you should live as becomes the Savior Who died for the church. Christian living in the world, in the final analysis, is nothing more or less than living in the world as a faithful member of a kingdom that is not of that world. May this study simplify and explain things for you and encourage you to do just that.

Other Titles by Dr. Jay Adams

available from your bookstore or
directly from TIMELESS TEXTS
1-800-814-1045

The Christian Counselor's Commentary Series
by Jay E. Adams   all volumes hardback

Vol. 1—I & II Corinthians
Vol. 2—Galatians, Ephesians, Colossians & Philemon
Vol. 3—I & II Timothy and Titus
Vol. 4—Romans, Philippians, and I & II Thessalonians
Vol. 5—Hebrews, James, I & II Peter, and Jude
Vol. 6—Proverbs
Vol. 7—The Gospel of John & The Letters of John and Jesus

> This series of commentaries is written in everyday
> English. A must for the layman as well as the Pastor/
> Counselor. Dr. Adams' everyman style of communica-
> tion brings forth these biblical truths in a clear under-
> standable way that typifies his writings. He does not try
> to duplicate the standard, more technical types of com-
> mentaries but supplements them with the implications of
> the text for God-honoring counseling and Christian liv-
> ing.

The Christian Counselor's New Testament
translated by Jay E. Adams   leather & synthetic bindings

> A special translation by Dr. Adams with extensive foot-
> notes and topical side columns. This Bible was specially
> designed to help the Christian in study as well as coun-
> seling. *The Christian Counselor's New Testament*
> is very user friendly. It leads you through those tough
> counseling topics by using the Margin Notations and
> Notation Index for the topic or related topics. Easily used
> during the counseling session.

A Call for Discernment—
Distinguishing Truth from Error in Today's Church
by Jay E. Adams   142pp. paperback

Dr. Adams shows the seriousness of the problem of lack of discernment and the effect on Christian lives. *A Call For Discernment* will help you become a more discerning Christian today.

Back to the Blackboard—
Design for a Biblical Christian School
by Jay E. Adams   160pp. paperback

With curriculum in the courtroom and parents up in arms, education is in the forefront of discussion in much of America today. Here is a truly provocative book on what qualifies as Christian education. These ideas are also very adaptable for the home schooler.

What to do on Thursday—
A Layman's Guide to the Practical Use of the Scriptures
by Jay E. Adams   144pp. paperback

The Bible has the answers, but can you find, understand and apply them? *What to do on Thursday* teaches you how to study and interpret your Bible to answer the questions that arise all week at work, at play, at home, and at school.

Dr. Adams has written this study to prepare you to meet the challenges of this fast-moving world with decisions that will honor God. The practical use of the Scriptures on an everyday basis is crucial to all of God's people. You can't wait for your pastor to preach a sermon that applies to your need now. *What to do on Thursday* will help you prepare a template of priorities that will order your life in a Godly pattern.

Teaching to Observe—The Counselor as Teacher
by Jay E. Adams   131pp. paperback

> Here is a book that is long overdue. Carl Rogers con-
> vinced a generation of counselors to listen and reflect
> while insisting that teaching is taboo. Though Rogerian-
> ism failed, and is now largely passé, many counselors
> still hesitate to teach their counselees.
>
> Dr. Adams shows not only that God obligates Christian
> counselors to teach, but how they may do so in ways that
> will help counselees both learn and "observe" those
> things that Christ "commanded" according to Matthew
> 28:20. He demonstrates clearly, using illustrations to
> which you will resonate, that effective biblical counsel-
> ing requires teaching. This book, the only one of its kind,
> is must reading for every serious Christian.

Winning the War Within—
                    A Biblical Strategy for Spiritual Warfare
by Jay E. Adams   151pp. paperback

> Christian, you are at war! It is the battles at two levels—
> one outward, the other inward—that are our responsibili-
> ties as members of the church. While the outer battle is
> vital and pressing, it cannot be fought as it should be
> unless the Christian is successfully winning the war
> *within*. Do you know how to fight the war within? This
> book—reflecting the spirit of the Word of God—has
> been written to tell you in no uncertain terms that there is
> a way to victory. And, avoiding the path of mere theory,
> it explains how you, no matter how many times you have
> been defeated in the past, can begin to consistently win
> the battles within.

A Thirst For Wholeness
by Jay E. Adams   143pp. paperback

> How healthy is your spiritual integrity? Do your actions speak so loudly that people won't listen? *A Thirst for Wholeness* provides the solution to this common problem. Drawing on the book of James, Dr. Adams concentrates on how you can become a complete Christian from the inside out. As you study the inner dynamics involved in this process, you'll learn how to get your spiritual beliefs and your everyday actions in sync.

The Grand Demonstration—
    A Biblical Study of the So-Called Problem of Evil
by Jay E. Adams   119pp. paperback

> Why is there sin, rape, disease, war, pain and death in a good God's world? Every Christian asks this question— but rarely receives an answer. Read this book and discover what God Himself says.

> *The Grand Demonstration* penetrates deeply into scriptural teaching regarding the nature of God. Moving into territory others fear to tread, Dr. Adams maintains that a fearless acceptance of biblical truth solves the so-called "problem of evil".